MUSIC
IN TEREZÍN
1941–1945

JOŽA KARAS

MUSIC
IN TEREZÍN
1941–1945

BEAUFORT BOOKS
PUBLISHERS
NEW YORK
in association with Pendragon Press

Copyright © 1985 Jŏza Karas

Library of Congress Cataloging in Publication Data

Karas, Jŏza.
   Music in Terezín 1941–1945.

   1. Music—Czechoslovakia—Terezín (Concentration
camp)—History and criticism. 2. Jews—Music—
Czechoslovakia—Terezín (Concentration camp)—History
and criticism. 3. Terezín (Czechoslovakia: Concentration camp)—History. I. Title.
ML247.8.T47K43   1985   780'.9437'1   84-24411

ISBN 0-8253-0287-0

Published in the United States by Beaufort Books Publishers, New
York, in association with Pendragon Press.

Printed in the U.S.A.   First Edition

10   9   8   7   6   5   4   3   2   1

To the memory
of
my late wife, Milada

Contents

List of Illustrations

The photographs included in this book are courtesy of the following: Memorial Terezin; Jewish State Museum, Prague; Yad Vashem, Jerusalem; Alice Shek; Karel Berman, Marie Bass; and Dr. H.G. Adler.

xiii

How This Book
Came Into Existence

In the beginning of 1970, as I started to think ahead—with some trepidation—to my otherwise unproductive summer months, I recalled reading three short articles in the Czech musical magazine *Hudební Rozhledy* (Musical Outlooks). According to them, eight short compositions and fragments of music which had originated in the Jewish concentration camp in Terezín were deposited in the archives of the Jewish State Museum in Prague. An idea struck me like lightning! Here was a perfect project for something worthwhile and interesting to do during the time of my involuntary leisure.

I found the three issues of the periodical and with great care read the aforementioned articles several times. The story had all the ingredients of a mystery, and I could be the sleuth who would unravel it. However, together with all the intrigue, a doubt came to my mind: if the history of the Holocaust had been a subject of a very close scrutiny, of many books, films, television programs, and scientific research, why had someone else not become interested in this inspiring facet of the Jewish life during the tragic years of World War II? Why should I, a Christian, get involved in a research project virtually untouched for twenty-five years, since the last puff of smoke had darkened the skies of Auschwitz? Putting aside these questions, I felt attracted to the project because I am a Czech musician, and this was a subject dealing with the music of Czechoslovak Jews. Little did I suspect that my modest summer project would occupy my mind night and day for the next ten years.

The first person to whom I mentioned the fact that some musical activities had existed in a Jewish concentration camp was my good friend and colleague Arthur Koret, cantor of the Emanuel Synagogue in West Hartford, Connecticut. He urged me immediately to look more closely into the matter and get more information. My subsequent correspondence with the Czechoslovak Music Information Center and my friend, Prof. Jan Kapr in Prague, not only corroborated the stories in the magazine, but led to a contact with Karel Berman, a former Terezín inmate and performer, thus indicating that the musical history of Terezín had a much broader basis. However, it became apparent at the same time that serious research could not be done by mail. Cantor Koret's excitement prompted me to seek financial assistance for a trip to Czechoslovakia, but skepticism about the unheard of cultural life in a Jewish concentration camp hindered any effort for a grant. In the meantime, my curiosity and interest grew as I obtained fascinating new information, but the bare reality just about forced me to reconcile myself to abandoning the project.

I felt jilted as I recounted my frustrations one day to my friend Ivor Hugh, then the Director of Cooperative Ministry of the Connecticut Council of Churches. I did not expect any help from him, since he was working on a limited budget, and besides, I was getting involved in a Jewish subject. To my astonishment, he expressed interest in using my findings on some of his radio and television programs, and promised to raise money for my trip. And he fulfilled his promise by taking—unknown to me—a personal loan!

And so, on Saturday, August 1, 1970, I found myself suddenly in Prague. Of course, I did some preparatory work ahead of time through my new contacts and mainly through my mother, Marie Karasová, who coordinated my activities and itinerary. The following Monday I paid a visit to the Music Information Center. Their official, Dr. Jarmila Pacovská, arranged two meetings for me right on the premises with the musicologist Dr. Ludmila Vrkočová, and with Prof. Eliška Kleinová, herself a Terezín survivor. The former gave me a copy of a chapter on music in the town of Terezín from her forthcoming book on the musical topography of Bohemia, and the latter immediately gave me an in-depth lecture on the musical life in the ghetto. At the conclusion, she put into my hands six original manuscripts of compositions written by her late brother, Gideon Klein, during his incarceration in Terezín. As I was staring incredulously at the treasure in my hand, she opened her briefcase once again and gave me five more scores of another Terezín inmate, Hans Krása, among them the piano reduction as well as the complete orchestral version of his children's opera *Brundibár*. Without asking for any receipt, she let me take all this music to my uncle, Oldřich Smola, to make photocopies.

On the following day, the Music Information Center provided me with a limousine for a visit to Terezín, in company of Mrs. Vrkočová. A member of the board of directors of the Terezín Memorial, Dr. Karel Lagus, also a fortunate survivor of the ghetto, readily answered my mushrooming questions and arranged for us a special guided tour of the premises. Then, very willingly, he made arrangements with the director, Václav Novák, on my behalf to obtain photocopies of any document which would enable me to get deeper insight into the conditions in the concentration camp.

Equally fruitful was my visit to the Jewish Museum in Prague on the next day. I received permission to make photocopies of the portfolio containing the eight pieces of music which started me on this quest, and again I obtained new documents and information in regard to the cultural life in the ghetto, mainly through the efforts of Dr. Anna Hyndráková.

And so it went. In the following days I visited Karel Berman in his summer home in Southern Bohemia; the widow of the composer Pavel Haas, Dr. Soňa Haasová, in the Moravian capital, Brno; and she in turn introduced me to Prof. Lubomír Peduzzi, author of a biography of her late husband. Back in Prague, I received additional valuable documents about Egon Ledeč from his nephew and my former classmate at the Prague Conservatory, Dr. Jan Ledeč, and from the officials of the Jewish Community Bureau in Prague, Dr. Rudolf Iltis and Arnošt Weiss; eventually somebody suggested that I visit Mrs. Marie Heřmanová. Her late husband, Karel Heřman, amassed, while in Terezín, some 380 programs, drawings, and autographed souvenirs, one of the most valuable sources of documentation of the cultural life in the ghetto. The visit proved to be a success, and I received permission to take pictures of any number of these documents.

In all my trips and errands, my brothers František and especially Zdeněk acted as my chauffeurs, secretaries, messengers, and all around helpers, and above all, my most welcome companions. During my entire visit in Czechoslovakia, everybody deluged me with kindness and assistance beyond my wildest dreams.

The overwhelming success of my trip affected the course of my action after my return home. Suddenly there was an immense amount of work to be done, organizing the material and transcribing some twenty scores, many of them almost illegible. Once more I embarked on the search for some grant which would free me from my regular obligations and permit me to devote myself to the project on a full-time basis. And once more my efforts were futile, because it sounded too farfetched and unreal to imagine extensive musical activities and even creativity in, of all places, a Jewish concentration camp. Finally, Ivor Hugh contacted Pamela Ilott, Director of Religious Broadcasts for CBS News, with the proposal to produce a television program based on my research. Her affirmative response resulted in a TV Special, "There shall be heard again . . . ," which appeared on the CBS Network on September 26, 1971.

In the meantime, I wrote a short essay about the musical activities in Terezín and also lectured on the subject for live audiences as well as on radio and television. Simultaneously, I came to the conviction that all the music from Terezín deserved to be recorded in some sort of memorial album for its historical value and its intrinsic artistic merit as well. On the advice of Frank Siegfried from Avantgarde Records, Ivor and I approached Benjamin Selvin, who has spent most of his life in the recording industry. By this time he was officially retired but busy as ever, especially since he had started his collaboration with Waldo Mayo, to whom he introduced us immediately. Both gentlemen became extremely interested in my project and plunged into work on my behalf. For me it meant gathering further information on the background of the composers from Terezín and their works written here.

As I was acquiring new data, I felt the need to write an extensive book dealing with the musical life in the Terezín ghetto. I did not consider myself competent to do so in a language which was not my mother tongue, especially since I had not written anything of substance even in Czech, except for an occasional newspaper article and a few English lectures on Czech music, which my late wife, Milada Javora, had so patiently corrected while enlightening me in regard to the mysteries and traps of the English language. Once, over lunch, I mentioned my dilemma to Arnold Forster, the General Counsel to the Anti-Defamation League of B'nai B'rith. He suggested that I talk to his friend Harold Flender, author of a number of books, and ask him to be my ghost writer. It was Harold who persuaded me to do my own writing, and gave me the promise that he would act as my editor. Neither one of us suspected at that time that he would not live long enough to fulfill his promise.

From the documents at my disposal I learned about a survivor of Terezín, Hedda Grab-Kernmayr, one of the busiest performers and organizers there. Apparently she lived somewhere in the western United States and could be an extremely valuable source of information. In order to find her whereabouts, I contacted another Terezín survivor, Marianne Zadikow May. She in turn got in touch with a friend, Eva Glaser, from Caracas, who sent me the address of Dr. Kurt Wehle of New York; he recommended that I write to Dr. H. G. Adler in London, the most knowledgeable person on the subject of Terezín.

I had already begun the work on my book and had completed several opening chapters and the epilogue. I had also received the first financial assistance in the form of two modest grants from the Connecticut Commission on the Arts and the Memorial Foundation for Jewish Culture. In this respect, Dr. Harry Barron from the

National Foundation for Jewish Culture proved to be of significant help. I had in my possession copies of more than twenty-five original compositions from Terezín, more than anybody ever suspected to exist. When I sent my first letter to Dr. Adler, I hoped for the requested address and perhaps a few minor details about the cultural activities in the ghetto. The address I did not obtain. As a matter of fact, I never located Hedda Grab-Kernmayr, and I doubt that I ever will. If she is still living, she is in her eighties. However, the "minor details" proved to be far from that. Dr. Adler informed me about his books on Terezín, his large collection of documents and, above all, more than twenty-five pieces of music composed in Terezín by Viktor Ullmann and Zikmund Schul.

Under these circumstances it would be foolish to continue with the writing of the book and also with the preliminary work for the intended recordings. Instead, more research, preferably on location, seemed to be imperative. My friends Waldo Mayo and Ben Selvin understood my needs and willingly subsidized my next trip to London with another visit to Czechoslovakia, to search for the new documents and additional information. And so, in the late summer of 1973, I found myself once more in Prague, this time armed with a tape recorder, talking to survivors of Terezín about their musical experiences in the ghetto.

Ten days later, I knocked on the door of the London apartment of Dr. Adler. His reception could not have been any friendlier or more cordial. I introduced myself in English, but my accent betrayed my origin, and he switched immediately to my native Czech. I spent the following ten days in London, visiting the Adlers' apartment daily. Dr. Adler gave me one entire room as a study and inundated me with his documents and musical scores. While he patiently answered my questions, his wife, Bettina, took care of my welfare by bringing me tea and other refreshments and inviting me frequently for dinner. Upon my return home, I had, besides my fondest memories of the stay in London, more material witnessing to the scope of the musical life in Terezín—more than I would ever have dreamed.

My new work consisted of organizing the recently acquired material and incorporating it into my previous findings, deciphering the handwritten documents, and transcribing the musical scores. I also hoped to resume writing of the book. All this had to be done in my spare time, since I had to attend to my ordinary obligations to support my large family. In the meantime, the health of my wife of twenty years deteriorated, and I had to take over the duties of a homemaker as well. When she passed away, after a long illness, in September of 1974, my research came to a virtual standstill, except for the American premiere of the children's opera *Brundibár*, which I conducted in the Hartford Jewish Community Center in April 1975. I was also able to conclude the translation of the opera into English, a task commenced several years before in collaboration with my wife. This time, my friend Bro Herrod lent me his helping hand in my undertaking.

The year 1976 signified a turn in my life and in my work as well. I remarried, and my wife, Anne Killackey, presented me with a most generous offer: to work on my research, while she would keep her full-time employment and thus provide for my whole family. At the same time, Waldo Mayo started a large fundraising project in West Palm Beach, Florida, for the benefit of the Ben Gurion University in Beersheva, Israel, in which he intended to utilize some of the music from Terezín. Unfortunately, this idea did not come to fruition, for he passed away unexpectedly in the summer of 1976. The loss of an interested friend and benefactor closed one avenue of my endeavor but simultaneously opened another door, even more important for the completion of my research and subsequently of this book. I was introduced to Waldo's sister, Lucille Schweitzer, and her lawyer, Carl Schaeffer. In memory of Waldo's last involvement, Mrs. Schweitzer subsidized my last research trip, leading this time to Israel with another stopover in Czechoslovakia.

The trip took place in the final days of 1976 and beginning of 1977. It was connected with an invitation from the Ben Gurion University, through the intercession of their American Associates, led by Aron Chilewich. All concerned made my journey not only most exciting but also extraordinarily successful. The moment I stepped off the plane in Tel Aviv, I was greeted by a young representative of the school, Eli Weiner, who prepared my itinerary for the first week and during that time acted as my very competent assistant. We visited, first of all, the kibbutz Givat Haim-Ihud, home of the Theresienstadt

Martyrs Remembrance Association and the museum Beit Terezín. The director of the museum, Pindă Shefa, very graciously showed me their collection and archives and made available any documents I was interested in. Interviews and meetings followed from Haifa in the north to a visit to the University in Beersheva in the desert. And wherever I went, I was always overwhelmed by the cordial reception and eagerness to assist me in my quest to preserve this history.

The second week of my visit to Israel I spent in Jerusalem. Eli had to leave me on my own, because of his sudden appointment to diplomatic service, but I was not left abandoned by any means. The assistant director general of the Ministry of Tourism, Max Vidar, native of Czechoslovakia, offered all necessary help to make my sojourn productive, and I often called him for advice in practical matters. A couple of times I even received an invitation to his home, where I met among others Zeev Shek, a vice-secretary at the Ministry of Foreign Affairs and later Israeli ambassador to Rome. It was Mr. Shek who granted me the most fascinating interview about the children's care in Terezín and provided me with his writings on the subject. (I was shocked to learn that both of these gentlemen died within the next two years, at a relatively young age, in their mid-fifties.)

Most of the daytime hours in Jerusalem I spent at the Yad Vashem Memorial or at the Hebrew University. From the former institution I obtained new acquisitions with the permission of the director, Dr. Josef Kermisz, while his senior assistant, Dr. Herbert Rosenkranz, arranged for me a special showing of the fraudulent movie produced by the Nazis in Terezín, and also helped me in contacts with various departments of Yad Vashem. The visit to the Hebrew University proved to be equally fruitful. They have in the archives an entire department of taped and transcribed interviews, made with the survivors of the Holocaust in the mid 1960s. Of special interest to me were the ones dealing with Terezín and, in particular, with the cultural life there. Again, I received permission to procure copies of these testimonies, which proved to be very useful. Then I spent the evenings interviewing further Terezín inmates from the ranks of performers as well as their audiences. And finally, I had the opportunity to meet the assistant president of the Ben Gurion University, Yakov Avnon, who was instrumental in all the arrangements connected with my stay in Israel.

One more stop in Prague resulted in obtaining some more information, and then, for the third time, I was facing the reorganization of all my material, old and new, into proper sequence and order, rewriting the previously finished chapters and working on the new ones. It took me almost another three years before I produced the final version, always verifying some conflicting data and filling still existing gaps in certain areas, mainly in the field of popular music. And once again, I received help from old and new friends and acquaintances, such as Václav Nelhybel, whom I consulted on my occasions in regard to the musical compositions, or his wife, Dorothy, who corrected some of my translations of German text into English. Max Bloch, a former student of Viktor Ullmann in Prague, shed light on some of the dark corners in his mentor's life and work, and Marie Krása Bass, sister of the composer, together with her late husband Hugo, transferred to me all the rights to Hans Krása's music. Finally, when all my writing was done, Dr. Kathleen McGrory, Vice President of the Eastern Connecticut State University, graciously undertook the task of editing my manuscript.

Finding a publisher for my completed book was much more difficult than I have ever imagined. After a couple of years of fruitless effort to submit the manuscript to a publisher directly and with the help of a literary agent, the newly appointed Dean of the Hartt School of Music of the University of Hartford, Donald Harris, contacted a few people on my behalf and then advised me to approach the Pendragon Press. The outcome was most gratifying and my quest came to the end. However, not my passion for the music of Terezín. In 1979, I formed my own string quartet for the purpose of performing the works, about which I could, hitherto, only lecture. My ultimate goal is to make the music sound in live performances and on recordings.

Reviewing the involvement of so many people in my project, do I have the right to call myself the author of this book? I used the knowledge and experiences of others, I formalized their statements, at other times I only transcribed their actual words or translated them from one language into another one, always trying to preserve the original flavor, even at the expense of elegant English. I would, therefore, call myself rather a co-author or a spokesman for all the aforementioned individuals and institutions and all the others who granted me interviews and furnished me with valuable information through correspondence. Their names appear in the bibliographical section of this book. To all of them I am greatly indebted for their collaboration, to all of them I am here humbly expressing my most sincere thanks and appreciation.

During the last eleven years I have met many wonderful people, I learned a lot about the subject of music produced and performed under the most unusual circumstances, and I gained a deeper insight into the spirit and character of my Jewish friends. My life has been tremendously enriched, and if I can pass this enrichment on to one single reader, I shall feel totally rewarded.

Bloomfield, Connecticut
October 16, 1981

Joža Karas

Prologue

On a dismal day, October 16, 1944, a freight train moved lazily from Terezín to an unknown destination somewhere in the East. Perhaps the sun was shining brightly, but it was dismal inside the cattle cars filled with a strange cargo. This was a normal sort of day, especially in the few weeks between September 28 and October 28 of that year, with a number of similar trains heading in the same direction, always with the same purpose: to transport thousands of prisoners from the "anteroom to hell" to the real hell in Auschwitz,[1] thousands upon thousands of people whose only "crime" was that they were born of Jewish parents.

Suddenly a piece of paper appeared in the air alongside the train, gliding slowly to the ground. A postcard with a terse message had been dropped from the cattle car with the hope that some bystander would put a stamp on it and mail it. And somebody did.

A few days later the postcard reached its destination. It expressed concern about several people:

---

[1]When referring to the concentration camp, the German name, Auschwitz, will be used, rather than the Polish name, Oświęcim, to indicate the Nazi involvement and responsibility.

Egon Ledeč. Drawing by Petr Kien.

Dear Olinka,

Sofie Fischer has promised me today that she will visit our mother frequently. All of us think today very much of Leouš and Klárča. Be well. Let the dear God protect you.

Love and Kisses
Egon

There was no concern expressed about the sender himself. Egon Ledeč, former assistant concertmaster of the Czech Philharmonic Orchestra, a fine artist and equally fine person, always worried about others and lent a helping hand wherever possible. For almost three years the sound of his beloved violin poured like a healing balm into the hearts of his fellows in misery, and only a few days earlier he had participated in the world premiere of a composition written for the Terezín orchestra. Today the composer, the conductor, and many members of the ensemble, together with hundreds of yesterday's audiences, were on their way to the fearsome Unknown. On a little postcard Egon Ledeč wrote his own most fitting epitaph, the last sentence of the last chapter of his life story. There were only a few more words to be added, but that he could not do personally. Next day, in Auschwitz, he was led from the station platform directly into the gas chamber.

ONE

Road to Terezín

It's an earthly paradise at a glance.
And this is the beautiful land,
The Czech land, my home!
(From the Czech National Anthem)

It is only about one hour's drive from Prague to Terezín. For some seventeen thousand "visitors" the round trip took up to three and a half years. They were the lucky ones. For the less fortunate it became a one-way trip.

State highway 8 runs north of Prague through the typical hilly Czech countryside, frequently passing small towns and villages. Eventually the hills, covered with woods and fields, level off into meadows, and suddenly a strange mountain appears like a huge bubble on the flat surface of the earth—Říp. According to legend this is the place where the patriarch Čech ended his long journey from the East with his clan in his search for a new settlement. Upon reaching the top of the mountain he could see the fertile land, meadows and forest—the "earthly paradise." His decision to strike roots here was hailed by his grateful followers, who named the country in his honor "Čechy." What a pity that he could not foresee all the tragedy which this land and its nation were to endure throughout their whole history! And what an irony that a stone's throw from Říp, in the middle of this "earthly paradise," Hell would open its gates some thirteen centuries later and swallow almost 140,000 innocent victims! Had he anticipated it, who knows to which part of the globe he would have led his tribe.

The dubious history of Terezín dates back to the year 1780. At that time Emperor Joseph II of the Austro-Hungarian Empire felt the need to protect his domain with a fortress to prevent a possible German hordes invaded the rest of the defenseless and abandoned him that it was the Hapsburg expansion which had destroyed Czech sovereignty in 1621 and held the Czech lands under its subordination for the next three hundred years. Thus he founded a garrison town with a fortress within walking distance, and called it *Theresienstadt*— "Theresa's Town"—or in Czech *Terezín*, in honor of his mother, Empress Maria Theresa. The town is located at the confluence of the rivers Labe (Elbe) and Ohře (Eger)[2] with a picturesque outline of the Bohemian Central Mountain Range in the background.

Rather uninteresting and dull with a square in the center and streets at right angles, Terezín is surrounded with ramparts which almost forbodingly form a huge star. It used to be called the "Big Fortress," and it can accommodate about six thousand inhabitants in private homes and army barracks. On the opposite bank of the river Ohře lies the actual stronghold, the "Small Fortress," replete with ground fortifications, storage rooms, and corridors. It had and still has the rare distinction that it never served its original purpose and instead was often used as a maximum security prison. Among its most noteworthy occupants was Gavrilo Princip, who perhaps unintentionally started the first world war by assassinating Archduke Francis Ferdinand d'Este in the streets of Sarajevo. And as matter of fact, the "Small Fortress" served as a military prison even after 1918. During the Nazi occupation it became one of the most horrible political concentration camps on record.

---

[2]The names in parentheses are the German translations of the Czech names.

So this was Terezín, the important part of the blueprint for the "final solution of the Jewish problem," which the Nazis prepared and executed with proverbial German thoroughness.

The tragedy of Czechoslovak Jews started in Munich. It was just a small link in Hitler's gigantic master plan to preserve Judaism only in museums. German and Austrian Jews became acquainted with the tactics of the "super race" long before the Nazi occupation of the so-called *Sudetenland*, the Czech territories alongside the German border, in the fall of 1938. In the Munich agreement Hitler promised the end of his expansionistic efforts and a lasting peace. So the Jews—the majority of them German-speaking—together with their shattered Czech fellows, left their homes and sought a refuge in the remaining crippled "new" Czechoslovakia. However, their hope for tranquillity did not last even half a year. On March 15, 1939 the German hordes invaded the rest of the defenseless and abandoned country and established the *Protectorate of Bohemia and Moravia* (the two western provinces of Czechoslovakia) while Slovakia—on Hitler's insistence—proclaimed itself an "independent" state one day earlier.

The new Protector, Konstantin von Neurath, wasted no time with the integration of the Czech lands into the Third Reich. In the case of Jews it meant the Decree of June 21, 1939 concerning Jewish property and the definition of the Nazi concept of "Jew." In a rapid sequence of events the Jewish inhabitants of the Protectorate were ordered to wear a yellow "Star of David" with the name *Jude* (Jew) on their clothes, their stores and businesses had to display prominently a sign reading "Jewish Establishment," and shortly afterwards these signs came down as the Germans confiscated Jewish property and gave it to their own people, who started to move into the Protectorate to prove how "German" it really was.

Immediately, in 1939, the Jews had to turn in their radios, and step by step they were denied all the so-called luxuries. By the end of 1941, they could not own or use furs, cameras, typewriters, skis, phonographs, or musical instruments and, later, even house pets. Their drab lives were constantly harassed by further ordinances, such as a ban on using telephones, attending theaters, movies, concerts, and sports events. The marked people had to do their shopping in specially designated stores, serving them only in very limited hours, and otherwise they were not permitted even a recreational walk in the park. Social contact with their "Aryan" friends became impossible; an exchange of greetings could result in a punishment for both parties. The Nazi ruthlessness knew no limits. By October 1941, the Czech Jews could not buy cigarettes, sugar, or fruit, and, from January 1942, newspapers. The educated people lost their jobs, and, if lucky, they found employment as manual workers. Their children were expelled from the German schools during the school-year 1939/40, from the Czech schools the following year, and all Jewish education ceased in 1942.

September 1941 signaled the beginning of a three-and-a-half-year silence of Jewish music in the Czech lands. Works of Jewish composers such as Mendelssohn, Mahler, and Schoenberg disappeared from the concert and radio programs and were banned together with non-Jewish compositions evoking patriotic or resistance sentiments. Obviously, the proscribed list was headed by two operas by Bedřich Smetana, *Libuše* and *The Brandenburgs in Bohemia*, and ended with the elimination of Offenbach's tunes from the hurdy-gurdies! The proverbial German thoroughness did not overlook even the tiniest detail.

Of course, the Jewish artists were equally excluded from performing in public, soloists as well as members of various ensembles. But silenced they could not be. In some cases the need for artistic expression drove them to take the risk and give a recital under a pseudonym. Thus the brilliant young pianist Gideon Klein played several times under the name Karel Vránek, and the versatile young artist Karel Berman assumed the name František Havlas to conduct the "Smetana" chorus in Jindřichův Hradec. In a public concert, on May 4, 1940, he introduced his own choral composition *Song*, and after the performance made a terse comment in his diary: "It really hurts—only the conductor could acknowledge the success."

Economic necessity forced one concert pianist, Carlo S. Taube, a former student of Busoni in Vienna, to seek employment as pianist

---

[3]*Holubovský* is a free Czech translation of the German *Taube* (pigeon).

4

with salon orchestras in Prague cafes. Under the name "Holubovský"[3] not only could he support his family at least for a while, but he even composed several small pieces. His last engagement before the imprisonment was in the concert cafe "Nizza," designed—for the time being—exclusively for the Jews, where he played together with the violinist Otto Sattler, percussionist Otto Neumann, and often as a duo pianist with Kurt Maier.

These clandestine musical activities were, however, in violation of the new laws and therefore quite dangerous not only to the Jewish performers but also to their Aryan organizers and patrons. Understandably, there were not many performances. Also the Jewish audiences could not attend any such performances without grave risk.

And so the Jewish musical life took another form: recitals and musical soirées in private apartments and suburban villas or in the remaining Jewish institutions. In Prague alone there were several meeting places, some of them with regular monthly programs, others just occasional; the number of listeners fluctuated between 25 and 80, and in certain locations, such as the Jewish orphanage, even 150. The curfew for Jews was set at eight o'clock in the evening, which often made it necessary for the people to stay overnight. Precautions had to be taken on arrival not to raise suspicion, and the visitors would enter the building individually or in couples during prolonged intervals. One such memorable event took place in the large villa, "Na Jezerce," owned by K. Blass. The guest artist of the overnight affair, Gideon Klein, performed there for the first time Brahms' *Concerto in B-flat Major*, accompanied by a second piano instead of an orchestra. The success was overwhelming. Klein therefore repeated the last movement as an encore; then he added the Scherzo, followed by the second movement and finishing with the first.

The much sought after young basso Karel Berman kept busy during the year 1941. On March 15 he sang Schubert's and Brahms' lieder and the "Biblical Songs" by Dvořák in the Eislers' apartment; on April 27 he participated in excerpts from Smetana's opera "The Bartered Bride" at Mr. Knöpfelmacher's, and in May and June he collaborated in the monthly recitals held in the apartment of Iček

Klement on Charles Square in Prague. Among the frequent performers there one could meet the violinist Karel Fröhlich, cellist Friedrich Mark, or the alto Hedda Grab-Kernmayr, suitably accompanied by pianists Eduard Herzog and Jan Hardek.

The field of chamber music was well served by a very fine violist, Bedřich (Fritz) Wachtel, the artistic soul of his own string quartet. Heinrich Taussig played the first violin and Wachtel's son, cello. Wachtel also organized and conducted the Jubal Choir, named in honor of the biblical "father of them that play upon the harp and the organs." In their last private appearance, Wachtel's quartet performed Mozart's *Eine kleine Nachtmusik*. Afterwards, Bedřich Wachtel was sent for a short stay in Terezín and then to Auschwitz, where his life ended abruptly.

As these concerts grew in number and popularity, the variety of music included not only the standard repertoire but new compositions as well. Viktor Ullmann thus had several of his works presented at one of the approximately monthly concerts in the apartment of Prof. Konrad Wallerstein, a former teacher at the *Deutsche Musikakademie* (German Academy of Music) in Prague, and son of the well known cantor of the Mayzl synagogue, Moritz Wallerstein. A formal printed announcement of one such concert, issued to the invited guests, reads as follows:

INVITATION

to a house concert at Prof. Konrad Wallerstein
Prague II., U Půjčovny 5/III
Sunday, March 3, 1940, at 5:00 P.M.

SONGS AND PIANO COMPOSITIONS
of Viktor Ullmann

Spiritual Songs, op. 20	Miss Margot Wallerstein
Sonata for Piano, No. 2, op. 19	Mrs. Alice Herz-Sommer
Hafis' Songbook (First Suite), op. 30	Mr. Robert Stein
From "Love Songs of famous women"	
Three Sonnets of Elizabeth Barrett	
Browning, op. 29	Mrs. Marion Podolier

Variations and Double-Fugue on
a theme by Arnold Schönberg,
op. 3 (revised edition)   Dr. Arnošt Latzko

At the piano: Composer

These private recitals were direct predecessors of a unique phenomenon, the vivid artistic and musical life in Terezín, witness to an unbelievable strength of the human spirit.

Perhaps it should be explained at this point how important a role culture in general and music specifically played in the life of the Central European intelligentsia. It was not a pastime, entertainment, social obligation, or fad to attend concerts and operatic performances. It was rather a way of life, an integral part, as important as basic human needs such as food and drink. Music education, limited in the schools only to the singing of folk songs often without any accompaniment and a few rudiments of theory, could not be separated from general education. But, of course, it had to be acquired privately. From the ranks of professional people emerged highly qualified amateurs, full-fledged performing artists, and even composers of extraordinary caliber. Instead of playing bridge, string quartets would meet for their weekly sessions with Haydn or Mozart, and individuals whose schedule permitted came home every day for lunch with a Beethoven sonata for dessert.

(To substantiate this assertion one can recall what happened in Austria shortly after World War II. Unlike the ancient Romans, who cried *"Panem et circenses"*—"bread and circuses"—in that order, the starved Austrians were primarily concerned with their heavily damaged Viennese opera house. The new independent government therefore allocated relief money not for the purchase of food but for the earliest possible restoration of the Temple of Euterpe.)

The harassment of the Jews took a turn for the worse in the summer of 1940, when the first Jewish concentration camp opened its gates at Lípa (Linden),[4] in southeastern Bohemia. The Germans called it *Umschulungslager* (training camp), because young Jewish men went there to learn a manual skill or trade. Among the prisoners were several professional musicians, such as the previously

[4]The names in parentheses are the German translation of the Czech names.

7

mentioned Karel Berman and Karel Frölich. They organized musical activities in free time, after their daily work. Their original efforts were on a modest scale and, without attempting to diminish the importance of their labor, they did not grow significantly, simply because the inmates did not stay in Lípa long enough. After several months they returned home, though not for long. The camp itself remained open, and after a while changed to a full-fledged concentration camp.

However unpleasant and difficult the life of the Jews in the Protectorate might be, it was still very far from the worst. That was yet to come. Come it did on September 27, 1941 in the person of SS-Obergruppenführer Reinhard Heydrich, who succeeded the so-called ailing von Neurath as Vice-Protector, but to whom his serfs would preferably refer as "The Hangman." How much the Jewish problem occupied Heydrich's mind could be determined from the fact that on October 10 he held the first meeting with Adolf Eichmann, Karl Hermann Frank, and several other SS officials. At that meeting they decided on the establishment of the Terezín ghetto, and exactly one week later, in a similar meeting, they worked out some of the details. The ghetto was to have a Jewish self-administration, responsible, of course, to the SS. For the first SS commander of Terezín, the Nazis had chosen the *Hauptsturmführer*, Dr. Siegfried Seidl. Then they ordered Jakob Edelstein, the former secretary of the socialist Zionist party, Paole Zion, to head the Council of Elders, and another Zionist leader, Otto Zucker, to be his deputy. Edelstein had been aware of concentration camps, such as Dachau, Buchenwald, or Auschwitz, and he sincerely believed that the establishment of Terezín would enable the Czech Jews to remain in Bohemia, and thus save them from transport to the annihilation camps. Little did he know that this arrangement would work quite differently. For example, the SS commander would order one thousand inmates to Auschwitz, and the Jewish administration had to select the victims.

And so, no matter how honorable Edelstein's intentions and expectations were, the fate of the Protectorate Jews was sealed, and the darkest chapter of Terezín history was about to begin.

TWO

The Earliest
Musical Efforts

I wander through Theresienstadt,
My heart a lump of lead.
The road all of a sudden ends,
Near where the fortress stands.
> Ilse Weber
> Terezín poet-composer

The forceful evacuation of the gentile population had hardly begun when the first Jewish transport arrived in Terezín on November 24, 1941. This group of 342 young men, many of them volunteers enticed by false promises of freedom and weekend trips home, was called the *Aufbaukommando* (building detail). They had the task of preparing the town for the new inhabitants. However, in their living quarters they met the first Nazi deceit: bare walls and empty floors in the so-called "Sudetenkaserne"

(Sudeten barracks).[5] Instead of beds and pillows, their own bags were under their heads, and for blankets overcoats had to do. And instead of the promised weekend trips home, they became the first prisoners of the Terezín "ghetto." Scarcely had they started working when two transports, each containing 1,000 people, came from Prague and Brno, on November 30 and December 2 respectively. Among the newly arrived were old persons, children, and the sick, and, not surprisingly, as early as the following day, the misery and hardship claimed its first fatality. It should be mentioned that already in October and early November, 5,000 Jews from the Protectorate preceded them in several transports heading for the concentration camps: Łódź in occupied Poland, and 1,000 for the Byelorussian Minsk.

On December 4, the second *Aufbaukommando*, with a thousand young men, engineers, physicians, technical and administrative personnel, and laborers, took up residence in Terezín. Many of them were also volunteers, persuaded by Jakob Edelstein, who came with them, accompanied by his staff of thirty-two. This was the original Council of Elders (*Ältestenrat*), and most of its members had been working previously for the Jewish Community Bureau in Prague. One can hardly imagine their shock when they realized that in Terezín they were merely puppets of the SS commander, Dr. Siegfried Seidl.

With every arrival of the new transports, the increasing population crowded the Terezín facilities more and more. Soon all the barracks had been filled from attic to basement, and, as individual families of the original inhabitants were leaving the town, new prisoners took their places. By September 18, 1942, the number of inmates reached its peak, 58,491, almost a tenfold multiple of the original population. Family life was destroyed when men, women, children, the elderly and sick were separated and assigned to various houses and barracks. Only a handful of the Elders had the privilege of living in more humane conditions. Under these circumstances it was obvious that the food supply was totally inadequate, hygienic conditions far

[5]Most of the Terezín barracks had names of German cities or provinces, i.e. Hamburg, Dresden, Magdeburg, Sudeten, etc.

below any acceptable standards, and medical attention extremely limited, in spite of the heroic efforts exerted by the Jewish management and physicians. It is, therefore, not surprising that people were dying in unbelievable numbers, sometimes more than 150 in one day. Most survivors of this ordeal were sent to meet their death in the gas chambers of Auschwitz and to other concentration camps. As a matter of fact, the first 1,000 left Terezín on January 9, 1942, heading for Riga. And so the transports kept coming and going. In the short history of the Terezín ghetto, between November 1941 and May 1945, a total of 139,654 people passed through its gates; 33,419 died there (16 of them executed for paltry reasons, such as sending a letter to relatives without permission), and 86,934 were deported, mainly to the East; 17,320 prisoners welcomed the liberation at the beginning of May, 1945. With some 2,000 people unaccounted for, the total of survivors who at one time or another lived in Terezín was about 20,000. Perhaps the most frightening part of these statistics is the inclusion of 15,000 children under the age of 15 years. Of those only about 1,000[6] ever "saw another butterfly."

The arrival of the first *Aufbaukommando* signaled the beginning of a cultural life unparalleled in the history of Western civilization. For its members not only took care of the physical needs of the incoming transports, but some of them also started catering to their spiritual necessities. Two men in particular are credited as initiators of the cultural activities: Karel Švenk (Schwenk),[7] a pioneer of the avant-garde theater in his native Prague, born March 17, 1907, and the excellent pianist and conductor Rafael Schächter, born May 17, 1905 in Romania, but raised and educated in Brno and Prague. However, other people claim precedence. Because most of the documents were written *ex post facto* and many of the involved artists did not survive the Holocaust, it is somewhat difficult to establish who really was responsible for these cultural activities. Apparently it was not an organized effort of a single person, but rather a spontaneous action by a number of artists, working individually or in groups.

[6]Most previous publications quote the number erroneously as one hundred.
[7]Many Czech Jews who bore German names repudiated them and changed them to Czech forms. Going through documents, one encounters various versions of the same name. Thus, Schwenk was the original German spelling.

Rafael Schächter. Drawing by Petr Kien.

Accordionist. Drawing by Bedřich Fritta.

Since there was no other diversion available, the men of the first *Aufbaukommando* spent their evenings in the barracks singing folk songs. Schächter took the initiative in leading the way. Shortly after, a number of young musicians from the second *Aufbaukommando*, who had met previously in the camp in Lipa, smuggled several smaller instruments into Terezín. The prisoners were allowed to take with them 50 kilograms (approximately 110 lbs.) of their most essential belongings, such as clothes, blankets, and food, but not musical instruments. For a professional musician an instrument is a bare necessity, and many of them took the risk of being caught. Karel Fröhlich brought in not only his violin but his viola as well, and his friend Kurt Maier, an accordion. There is even a story about a resourceful cellist who dismantled his cello into a few pieces of wood, wrapped them into a blanket together with some glue and clamps, and, once in Terezín, reassembled the instrument and began to play again. It is also plausible that the SS looked with a certain amount of benevolence on the *Aufbaukommando*, because its numerous members had volunteered for the job, and therefore searched their suitcases and knapsacks more leniently.

The first document about a musical program is dated December 6, 1941,[8] only two days after the arrival of the second *Aufbaukommando*. A variety show took place in the evening in the hall Number 5 of the "Sudeten" barracks. The participants were listed as follows: Proskauer—Master of Ceremonies; Karel Fröhlich and Heini (Heinrich) Taussig—violin; Viktor Kohn—flute; Wolfi Lederer and Kurt Meyer[9]—accordion; Fritz Weiss, Hans Selig, Pavel Kohn, Fredy Mautner, Franta Goldschmidt, Tedy Berger, Wolfi Lederer—Jazz Orchestra; Dr. J. Běhal and Franta Kraus—recitation; and Lewin—magician. Stage manager was Tonda Rosenbaum. The conspicuous absence of Schächter's name can be easily explained: he could not possibly prepare an organized chorus in such a short time, nor had he a piano at his disposal.

The violinist, Karel Fröhlich, with the accordionist, Kurt Maier, started their musical activities right from the outset of their sojourn

[8]Kurt Maier puts the date more realistically in the middle of December. The program had been typed belatedly after the performance.
[9]Correct spelling of the name is Maier.

13

in Terezín by playing for other inmates in their habitations, be it an attic or a basement in the barracks. As new transports kept on arriving in Terezín, additional artists joined the ranks of the impromptu performers, and so by Christmas of the same year, Egon Ledeč comforted his brothers in misery with the soothing sounds of his violin. By that time, the Nazis had found out about these illegal performances, but they did not forbid them. On the contrary, on December 28 they sanctioned these so-called *Kameradschaftsabende* (evenings of fellowship) and thus encouraged their rapid upsurge. The rationale behind this surprising reaction was that in this way the prisoners would not cause unnecessary trouble.

As Schächter's choral activities became more organized, he joined his talents with those of Karel Švenk, and early in 1942 they produced their first all-male cast cabaret or variety show. Before the war, Švenk was active in Prague and other Czech towns as actor, director, writer, and composer. He learned to react in his work to the political and sociological events in his environment, and this experience he brought to Terezín. No wonder, therefore, that, as a part of the variety show, he prepared a satirical sketch on a very fitting topic about a lost food card, something his audiences could easily identify with. The success was instantaneous, especially when the final song, the "Terezín March," reached the ears of the listeners. Its refrain expresses the cruel present and hope for the future:

> Everything goes, if one wants,
> United we'll hold our hands.
> Despite the cruel times
> We have humor in our hearts.
> Every day we go on
> Moving back and forth,
> And can write letters in only thirty words.
> Hey! Tomorrow life starts over,
> And with it the time is approaching,
> When we'll fold our knapsacks
> And return home again.
> Everything goes, if one wants,

United we'll hold our hands
And on the ruins of the Ghetto we shall laugh.

Coupled with a catchy marching melody, the text had all ingredients to become the prisoners' anthem in no time. Švenk then incorporated the "Terezín March" into all his subsequent cabarets. Unfortunately, the two great optimists did not live to laugh in May 1945.

Another boost to the budding cultural life in Terezín was given with the arrival of the transport on December 17, 1941 in the person of a very experienced and equally energetic operatic singer, the alto Hedda Grab-Kernmayr. While she had expected only the worst, she was fortunate enough to spend the whole war in Terezín making music. Of course, at the beginning of her stay there, she had to participate in lowly obligations, such as peeling potatoes, but her field of activities soon changed. As the running of the ghetto, under the leadership of Jakob Edelstein, became more and more efficient, the need of food for the soul became more apparent. So one day Edelstein's assistant, rabbi Dr. Erich Weiner, accompanied by the young educator Fredy Hirsch, visited Hedda Grab-Kernmayr and asked her to organize cultural activities, educational as well as entertaining programs, music, lectures, etc. This, together with the previously permitted *Kameradschaftsabende*, was in reality the beginning of the highly organized *Freizeitgestaltung* or Administration of Free Time Activities. Later, in 1942, this organization came into existence officially and was sanctioned by the SS command. Rabbi Weiner was named its first director, and the name of Hedda Grab-Kernmayr does not appear among the administrative personnel. However, she remained in Terezín until the liberation in May 1945 as one of the busiest performers.

The establishment of the *Freizeitgestaltung* was, of course, a very important achievement, because, from then on, all cultural activities were done with German approval, although sometimes they were subject to Nazi censorship. As "employees" of the *Freizeitgestaltung*, the artists and scientists were excluded from manual work and thus could, to a certain degree, pursue their career. This was especially

Freizeitgestaltung:

K/0	Leitung	Moritz Henschel
K/10	Administrative Leitung	Rabb. Dr. Weiner
K/11	Sekretariat	Dr. Hans Mautner
K/12	Programmbearbeitung	Anna Zelenka
K/13	Finanzgeb. u. Eintrittskart.	Dr. Georg Kohn
K/14	Bezirksarbeit	
K/15	Probenplan	Anna Zelenka
K/20	Technische Abteilung	Otto Spektor
K/21	Materialbeschaffung	Dr. Zd. Winter
K/22	Entwurf u. Dekoration	Architekt Franz Zelenka
K/23	Säleverwaltung	Dr. Friedner Hans
K/30	Theater	Kamill Hoffmann
K/31	Deutsches Theater	Curt Weisz
K/32	Tschechisches Theater	Gustav Schorsch
K/34	Kabarett	Kurt Gerron
K/35	Blockveranstaltungen	Myra Strauss
K/40	Musiksektion	Hans Krasa
K/41	Opern- u. Vokalmusik	Rafael Schächter
K/42	Instrumentalmusik	Gideon Klein
K/43	Kaffeehausmusik	Paul Libensky
K/44	Instrumentenverwaltg.	Paul Libensky
K/50	Vortragswesen	Dr. Franz Kahn
K/51	Allgemeine Vorträge	Prof. Dr. Emil Utitz
K/52	Jüdische Vorträge	Dr. Franz Kahn
K/53	Fremdsprachige Vorträge	Prof. Dr. Max Adler
K/54	Hebraika	Prof. Kestenbaum
K/55	Schach	Isidor Schorr
K/56	Frauenvorträge	Hana Steiner
K/60	Zentralbücherei	Prof. Dr. Emil Utitz
K/61	Allgemeine Abteilung	
K/62	Jüdische Abteilung	
K/63	Hebräische Abteilung	
K/64	Fachliteratur	
K/65	Bibliophile Abteilung	
K/70	Sportveranstaltungen	Dr. Zdeněk Winter
K/71	Fussball	Ota Hermann
K/72	Volleyball	Gustav Straschitz
K/73	Handball	Franz Kohn
K/74	Basketball	Rudolf Klein
K/75	Tischtennis	Kurt Löbl

List of the officials of the *Freizeitgestaltung*.

Poster of the *Freizeitgestaltung* signed by Hedda Grab-Kernmayr.

advantageous to young budding artists who were allotted time for practicing and studying, and for composers and writers creating new works. This in itself is extremely significant, because it was happening at the time when the rest of Europe and all occupied territories were completely cut off from any Jewish utterance. The explanation for this sudden tolerance on the side of the Nazis is that they considered the Terezín—and all—Jews as good as dead at a time when the extermination camps in the East were already in full operation. And while the Nazi attitude was, "Let them have their fun; tomorrow they will no longer exist," for the culture-thirsty prisoners this was the opportunity for the expression of defiance through artistic means. The importance and popularity of these cultural events among the Terezín inmates is further evidenced by the fact that several times in the history of the ghetto, the Nazis withdrew the performing privileges for a short period of time in reprisal and as punishment for attempted escapes and similar misdemeanors.

The entire administration of the *Freizeitgestaltung* comprised many departments, such as Czech and German theater; cabaret; a large music section with subdivisions for vocal, instrumental, and popular music; lectures; programing; scheduling of performances and practicing; technical department; chess; library; various sports, etc. The functionaries of the music section were also responsible for bringing into Terezín musical instruments, sheet music, and books from the confiscated Jewish possessions, stored in the Prague synagogues. Under these circumstances, Hedda Grab plunged into her work, and on March 21, 1942 she presented her first cultural program in the women's barracks at three o'clock in the afternoon. It included some reading and recitation, dance, and two "Biblical Songs" by Dvořák, sung by Hedda Grab-Kernmayr herself, and two lieder by Schubert, performed by Emmy Zeckendorf. Edelstein attended the presentation with his entourage, and that in itself was a minor miracle, because men were not permitted to visit women's barracks and vice-versa. The program was so successful that it had to be repeated several times not only in the women's barracks but in the men's as well.

The seriousness with which Hedda Grab accepted her new challenge is corroborated by the dates of her following presentations. *Pürglitzer Abschiedsprogramm* (Pürglitzer farewell program) took place on April 4. It is not known whether this production was connected in any way with the departures of transports from Terezín to the concentration camps in Poland during the month of April, comprising six thousand men, of whom only forty survived. The program itself was very cheerful and included several arias, dances, humorous *chansons,* and a marionette sketch. On May 3, the *Ghetto Lullaby* of Carlo Taube was presented within the framework of his *Ghetto Suite*, and then on June 5, in celebration of Theodor Herzl. The celebration of Theodor Herzl. The first fully vocal concert was performed in the courtyard of the "Hamburg" barracks on June 11, 1942. The participating artists, Gerta Harpmann, Jakob Goldring, Emmy Zeckendorf, Anka Dub, and Hedda Grab-Kernmayr, sang arias by Puccini, Meyerbeer, Bizet, Smetana, and Dvořák, as well as Yiddish songs, without any accompaniment. Then, fourteen days later, they repeated the same program in the "Magdeburg" barracks with Wolfi Lederer playing the accordion.

No opportunity was left unaccounted for in bringing to their fellow inmates a little beauty, diversion, even laughter, to make them forget for a fleeting moment the harsh realities of everyday life. At the same time, every utterance, no matter how modest, was accepted with the greatest possible gratitude.

THREE

Development of
Choral Activities

With the influx of prisoners to Terezín, Rafael Schächter's choral activities grew in scope and quality. The original informal singing of folk songs changed with the arrival of the pianist Gideon Klein. His pianistic abilities could not be utilized at the beginning of his sojourn in Terezín, where he came early in December 1941, because there was no instrument available. So he turned his attention to his previous interest, composition.

Gideon Klein was born in the Moravian town of Přerov, on December 6, 1919. At the age of eleven, he came to Prague to take liberal arts courses at the Jirásek Gymnasium simultaneously with intensive private studies of the piano. In the fall of 1938, while the menacing clouds of Nazism were casting their shadows over the Czechoslovak Republic, Klein entered the Master School of the Prague Conservatory as a student of Prof. Vilém Kurz, and at the same time he registered at the Charles University to undertake the studies of philosophy and musicology. After only one year in the newly established Protectorate, Klein graduated from the Master School, playing with great success Beethoven's *Piano Concerto* No. 4.

Poster for the opera *The Bartered Bride* by Bedřich Smetana.

His university studies came to an abrupt end a little later, on November 17, when the Nazis closed all institutions of higher learning in the occupied Czech territories. During the following year, Klein pursued the study of composition as a private student of Prof. Alois Hába and, at the same time, he concertized as much as the circumstances permitted. The star of the young artist was ascending rapidly on the Czech musical horizon, only to be eclipsed by his incarceration in the concentration camp.

Schächter found in Klein a collaborator par excellence. At first, Klein arranged Czech, Slovak, Hebrew, and even Russian folk songs for Schächter's ever expanding choral group. After the original all-male ensemble, Schächter formed a women's chorus, and the two combined logically into a mixed choir. In a program of the two choirs led by Schächter, thirteen out of fifteen Czech and Hebrew folk songs were arranged by Gideon Klein and only the remaining two by Bernard Pollak. The only existing piece from that program is the Hebrew song *Bachuri leantisa*, which Klein arranged for a three-part female chorus on December 3, 1942. Unfortunately, even this score is not complete, since the lyrics are omitted except for the first four measures.

The next logical step in Klein's artistic development was toward his own original composition. His affinity with Leoš Janáček is apparent from a composition for a male chorus on a text of Czech folk poetry, written in 1942, while the two "Madrigals" for five-part mixed chorus show his international orientation. One came into existence in 1942 and was based on the Czech translation of a text by François Villon; the other was composed in 1943 to the translated text of Friedrich Hölderlin.

Through the intercession of the *Freizeitgestaltung*, Schächter was able to secure a small room in the basement of the "Sudeten" barracks for his rehearsals. There he also conceived the idea of studying the choruses from the opera *The Bartered Bride* by Bedřich Smetana. According to the testimony of Hedda Grab-Kernmayr, she gathered for him a group of girls and lent him her pitch-pipe—the only available "musical instrument." The situation improved when Schächter obtained a broken-down reed organ and a half-broken accordion. From the choral parts of the opera it was only a step to a production of the entire work, since a number of acceptable soloists could be found in Terezín. In the gymnasium hall called "Sokolovna," just outside the town limits, somebody discovered a battered old baby-grand piano without legs. It had to be moved clandestinely into the ghetto at night, and was placed in the gymnasium of the school that housed boys. The task done, the operatic season was ready to be launched.

The festive premiere of *The Bartered Bride* took place on November 28, 1942.[10] Schächter simultaneously played the piano and conducted an excellent cast comprising Truda Borger as Mařenka, Franta Weissenstein as Jeník, Bedřich Borges in the role of Kecal, and Jakob Goldring as Vašek. The supporting roles were sung by Karel Polák, Hedda Grab-Kernmayr, Walter Windholz, Marta Tamara-Zucker, and a few others. The success of the opera was, understandably, enormous, since *The Bartered Bride* is the most typical Czech opera in the entire repertoire; as such, it holds an absolutely prominent place in the heart of every Czech music lover. Listeners of all ages had tears in their eyes upon hearing the opening chorus, "Why shouldn't we rejoice." The response was overwhelming, so overwhelming that the opera had to be repeated about thirty-five times. The already excellent production was even further enhanced when Marion Podolier took over the role of Mařenka, and the magnificent Karel Berman replaced the enthusiastic amateur Borges as Kecal for no less than twenty-five performances.

Hedda Grab, one of the performers, felt that the impression of the opera was unforgettable, while the writer Egon Redlich wrote in his memoirs that "this performance was the finest one that I have ever seen at the ghetto."[11] No less enthusiastic were the younger critics. A thirteen-year-old girl heard a performance of *The Bartered Bride* later, in 1943. In her diary she wrote:

> On the next day, we went to the gymnasium, L 417, filled to the last space. I found a spot next to the piano. I have heard *The Bartered Bride* three times in Prague, but it was never so beautiful as here. It is indeed a miracle that conductor Schächter was able to prepare it like that.

[10]Some sources put the date three days earlier.
[11]From the diary of Egon Redlich; used with permission of the Memorial Terezín.

When I was walking home and overheard all the small talk about food, black marketing, passes, and work in the fields, I felt like a person having beautiful dreams, who awakens suddenly, and everything is again trite as always. I was thinking all the time about *The Bartered Bride*, and even in my half-slumber I heard in my head: "Faithful loving."[12]

Following Schächter's example, other musicians organized singing groups according to the voices and also to their musical interests and preferences. Karel Berman became a conductor of a girls' chorus. As such, they sang the regular repertoire, consisting mainly of music by Czech composers, i.e., Dvořák's *Moravian Duets*. As a *voice band*, they recited gems from the Czech literature. The young and the young-at-heart welcomed their interpretation of the very popular Czech fairy tales written by the beloved author Božena Němcová, which the group presented in musical collaboration with Dr. Karel Reiner. Rudolf Freudenfeld[13] continued his association with his children's choir that had begun previously in a Jewish orphanage in Prague. Later, in 1943, came Karel Vrba, a musical amateur, who, besides joining Schächter's chorus, directed a boys' choir and organized also his own small male group, containing about ten men. They sang mostly folk songs, very often in Vrba's own arrangement. Siegmund Subak from Vienna formed the Subak Chorus specializing in Jewish liturgical music, Yiddish folk songs, and new Palestinian music. Somewhat similar was the Tempel Chor (Temple Chorus), apparently designed to participate in the religious services. Another group, counting about ten members, The Durra Chorus, bore the name of its leader and performed folk songs of various nationalities.

Very little is known about the activities of the aforementioned groups, whose existence is documented through extant posters. Some of them sang mainly for their own enjoyment and for the most immediate neighborhood.

In contrast to these are the activities of the Viennese composer-conductor Franz Eugen Klein, who conducted operas in the German language in Terezín, and Karl Fischer, who turned his attention to the field of oratorio. Both were artists of a high caliber, and their

---

[12]The famous love duet from the opera.
[13]After the war he changed his name to Franěk.

work received enthusiastic reviews from Viktor Ullmann as well as a warm reception from their audiences. Besides all the previously mentioned conductors, there were others who got the chance to wield the baton only occasionally but nevertheless successfully.

Final Chorus from Smetana's opera *The Bartered Bride*.
Autograph by Rafael Schächter.

FOUR

Opera in Terezín

While Smetana's ever popular *The Bartered Bride* continued to delight the enthusiastic Terezín audiences, Rafael Schächter began preparations on another opera of the same composer, *The Kiss* (*Hubička*). There is a considerable similarity between the two works; both are comic operas inspired by folk traditions depicting life in a Czech village, and both are influenced musically by the elements of Czech folk songs and dances.

Schächter assigned all the roles to the soloists so well proven in the first opera, with only one exception, Karel Polák, in the secondary role of Matouš. Once again, the opera was presented only in concert form with a piano accompaniment. The premiere took place in the attic of the "Dresden" barracks on July 20, 1943. Karel Berman recalls singing the opera fifteen times, presumably the total number of Terezín performances.

Schächter ventured into a Mozartian repertory comprised of the operas *The Marriage of Figaro* and *The Magic Flute*. The roster of singers shows several new names, some of them very distinguished. By the time *The Magic Flute* was in preparation, Machiel Gobets, the lyric tenor from the Netherlands Royal Opera, had joined the ranks of Terezín artists, and the elderly but still excellent coloratura Ada

Hecht exchanged the stage of the Viennese Volksoper for the limelight in the Terezín attics. Karel Ančerl described her rendition of Queen of the Night as absolutely fantastic. However, as a whole, the opera did not reach the splendid standard of Schächter's Czech operas. *The Magic Flute* has a very large number of roles, all of which require the finest voices and a thorough understanding of Mozartian style. This was more than the conditions in Terezín could offer, when several of the minor roles had to be entrusted to amateurs or even children. Furthermore, in the opinion of Viktor Ullmann, Rafael Schächter's forte did not lie in the interpretation of Mozart's operas. At the conclusion of his review, Ullmann claimed that the only opera by Mozart which could be properly presented under the existing conditions would be *Bastien and Bastienne*. Apparently the audiences in Terezín were not so critical, since Karel Berman, who alternated with J. Fried in the role of Sarastro, himself sang in seven performances.

The only opera conducted by Schächter (incidentally his last), which had been fully staged, was *La Serva Padrona* by Giovanni Battista Pergolesi. The wonderful soprano Marion Podolier found a surprisingly worthy counterpart in Bedřich Borges, and they were joined by Karel Švenk in the mute role of Vespone. The versatile Karel Berman tried his hand in the lively production as stage director on the sets designed by František Zelenka. The opera was performed with the full accompaniment of a string orchestra and continuo. A preserved poster from Terezín lists Hans Krása as cembalist. However, this is categorically disputed by Karel Berman, according to whom the continuo part was played on the piano by Schächter himself.

Several other conductors followed Schächter in his operatic endeavors. Among them the most prominent was the young Franz Eugen Klein, formerly the second conductor (*Kappelmeister*) of the Viennese State Opera. In Terezín he chose three pillars of the operatic repertory: Verdi's *Rigoletto*, Puccini's *Tosca*, and Bizet's *Carmen*. While Schächter represented the Czech opera, Klein was the exponent of the German one. It has to be understood that in Europe the operas were sung in the national languages rather than in the originals. Therefore, even though the operas conducted by

Klein were Italian or French, in Terezín they represented the German opera. Since most of the singers took part in all productions, it was not unusual to hear, in one performance, two or even three different languages. *Rigoletto* and *Tosca* enjoyed multiple performances with a double cast in 1943. The enthusiasm of the performers can be seen from a letter of the young basso, Otto Abeles,[14] to his sweetheart, Bohuslava Dostálová:

> As to my work here, I am always engaged in *Rigoletto*—it will be performed for the fourth time now. In a fortnight, there will be the first night of *Tosca* in which I have got but a small role—but never mind. Afterwards I'll sing or, better, study the part of the Comtur in Mozart's *Don Giovanni*—which, I hope, will suit me perfectly.
>
> I have plenty of work now: next week I have on my program the short but very gratifying part of the Count Monterone in *Rigoletto*, afterwards the role of the fretful gardener in *The Marriage of Figaro*, and still another in the *Tosca*—the one of Cesare Angelotti, small but significant. In addition to all that, I am preparing my own recital of songs and ballads, and precisely Löwe's *Archibald Douglas* and some lieder by Schubert and Schumann. This all shall be in about six to eight weeks . . .
>
> Darling, I must say that now we are working hard at the music here. Imagine—we are preparing *The Bartered Bride*, even with all the chorus numbers. I am singing Father Krušina. It will be lovely—what a great pity that you cannot be here! My soul is missing you so much at such moments, how much lovelier it would be if I could see you listening to my singing and sharing with me the delight in these divine strains![15]

Carmen was introduced to the Terezín audiences in 1944, after the arrival of the transport from the Netherlands, as witnessed by the presence of two participating artists, Kurt Gerron and Machiel Gobets. In contrast to *Tosca* and *Rigoletto*, *Carmen* was fully staged on modernistic sets of František Zelenka, and directed by Gerron. The orchestral accompaniment was replaced by two pianos, played by

---

[14]After the war he changed his name to Ambroz.
[15]From the diary of Egon Redlich.

29

Poster for the opera *Carmen* by Georges Bizet.

Edith Steiner-Kraus and Franz Eugen Klein, who also conducted. The star-studded double cast reads like a "Who's Who" of Terezín and included Gobets and David Grünfeld as Don Jose, Hedda Grab-Kernmayr and Ada Schwarz-Klein in the role of Carmen, Walter Windholz and Karel Freund as Escamillo, and in the secondary roles Karel Berman, Ada Hecht, Truda Borger, Hilde Aronson-Lindt, and others. *Carmen* was received with enthusiasm by the public as well as by the usually severe critic Viktor Ullmann, who, after a lengthy philosophic and aesthetic introduction, addressed himself in his review of the performance in the following manner:

> The singing in our production is rather praiseworthy. Grab-Kernmayr, Gobets, and Windholz offer splendid voices and spirited performances. The tightly prepared ensemble sections surprise pleasantly, among the smugglers especially Karl Fischer [sic!] and Pollak, with the ladies, Borger and Lindt. Mrs. Hecht, the ever ready artist, sings now all the soprano repertoire and is admirable in her versatility. The choruses are still as heavy as before and, although prepared with good precision, they sound somewhat laborious and not always satisfactory.
>
> Altogether, the presentation is an important achievement of the talented conductor, F. E. Klein. Problematic remains only the staging. If it goes half-way, it could go all the way. If it remains in the rehearsal stage, can one not come to the thorough enjoyment, especially, when one will be reminded far too much of Fritta's[16] spirited cartoons. But then I miss again Escamillo's umbrella.
>
> The climax of our production is reached, without any doubt, in the third act, in which, indeed, Bizet tied the dramatic knot with the hand of a Master. Here, Frasquita and Mercedes (Borger and Lindt) sing their charming duet, here Micaela (Hecht) permits us to to hear her breathtakingly sung arias, here Hedda Grab and Mr. Gobets display their voluminous and lush voices, here even the choruses grow to a satisfactory sonority.[17]

[16]Fritz (Bedřich) Fritta was one of the artists imprisoned in Terezín. His real name was Fritz Taussig.

[17]The reviews of Viktor Ullmann are used with the permission of Dr. H. G. Adler, owner of the entire collection. Translations by the author.

Karl Fischer, whose efforts gravitated to the field of oratorio, joined the ranks of operatic conductors with a concert version of *Cavalleria Rusticana* by Pietro Mascagni and Verdi's *Aida*. Eventually, Karel Berman also decided on a debut as operatic conductor. For his vehicle he selected a one-act comic opera of a Czech composer, Vilém Blodek, called *In the Well* (*V studni*). Due to unexpected circumstances, the opera received only one performance. According to Berman, in the midst of preparations, one Monday at noon an announcement was made by the SS headquarters that starting on the following Thursday, all public utterances would have to be in German. Having the hopes and efforts of many hours of work with the Czech text dashed by a single announcement might have dismayed less staunch hearts, but this was not so in Terezín, where hardship was the daily order. After a full day's work on Monday, all the participants gathered at night to work with more intensity than ever before. And practice they did, as a matter of fact, through the entire night. Tuesday was a regular workday, so they worked. And after a meager supper, they spent another sleepless night getting ready for the premiere. Then, after another full day of work, the festive performance took place on Wednesday night. The deadline had been met, the German clock was beaten, and for one short evening the losers became winners! The spirit would not yield to bodies completely exhausted.

Questionable, to say the least, was the choice of the operetta *Die Fledermaus* by Johann Strauss. The initiative for this undertaking came from a young talented musician, Wolfgang Lederer, who assembled for the production a cast worthy of any operettistic stage: the experienced singer-actors Anny Frey, Nella Eisenschimmel, Lisl Hofer, Kurt Weisz, Harry Hambo, Hans Hofer, and others. Adolf Aussenberg created the attractive scenery, and Eva Kohner was responsible for the colorful costumes. Since Lederer did not have an orchestra at his disposal, he solved the problem by entrusting the brilliant pianist Renée Gärtner-Geiringer, with the accompaniment, in which she cleverly alternated with a reed-organ, effectively imitating woodwind instruments.

The foremost authority on the life and conditions in Terezín, Dr. H. G. Adler, felt very strongly that opera in general was too extravagant in the concentration camp, and as such hardly had a place there. For that reason, he never attended any such performances, even though he was not only an ardent music lover but a musicologist as well. A presentation of an exuberant, light-hearted German operetta he all but condemned. Less harsh was Dr. Adler's friend Viktor Ullmann, in his extensive review. While he equally disagreed with the presentation of a German operetta, the reason was his preference for some work of a neglected—in Terezín—Jewish composer, Jacques Offenbach. At the end of his otherwise laudatory review, he encouraged Lederer to channel his future efforts in that direction.

In sharp contrast to offerings so remote to the life of Terezín, several imprisoned artists produced works in which they reacted and protested not only their personal lots but the world situation in general. A very talented young painter and poet, Peter Kien, wrote the libretto to an opera *Der Kaiser von Atlantis oder der Tod dankt ab* (*The Emperor of Atlantis, or Death Abdicates*), and Viktor Ullmann composed the very effective music.

In this highly allegorical story, Emperor Überall rules the corrupt and wicked Empire of Atlantis. When he orders the personified Death to lead his army into a war for his own glorification, Death refuses to do so and goes on strike, thus allowing no one to die. Chaos follows, and the Emperor realizes his own mistake. In exchange for Death's return to duty, the Emperor must become his first victim.

From the first note, Ullmann indicated that the work reflects unmistakably the situation under which it came into existence. He opens the opera with a trumpet call quoting the Death theme from the symphony *Asrael* by the Czech composer Josef Suk. ("Asrael," meaning "The Angel of Death," was the artistic reply and reaction of the composer after he lost, in rapid succession, his beloved mentor and father-in-law, Antonín Dvořák, and his own wife, Dvořák's daughter. The symphony was then performed on various occasions in connection with the death of prominent people, a national tragedy, etc., and was known as such to the music-oriented audiences.) The style of Ullmann's opera is reminiscent of that of Kurt Weill, with some of the musical numbers written in the jazz

Sketch of the set for Viktor Ullmann's opera, *The Emperor of Atlantis.*

idiom. The political connotation is explicitly expressed by the use of the Nazi anthem, *Deutschland, Deutschland über alles*, in a minor key variation, and the opera ends with an adaptation of Martin Luther's celebrated chorale *Ein' feste Burg ist unser Gott* (*A Mighty Fortress Is Our God*).

Der Kaiser von Atlantis was scored for five singers and a thirteen-piece orchestra. Ullmann wrote it having in mind special artists: Karel Berman as Death; Walter Windholz as Emperor; David Grünfeld, Pierrot; Marion Podolier in the role of the Girl; and Hilde Aronson-Lindt as Drummer. The orchestra included, together with the usual instruments, a saxophone, banjo, and harpsichord. (This would corroborate the presumption that a harpsichord had been brought into Terezín most likely for the performance of *La Serva Padrona*.) *Der Kaiser von Atlantis* was being readied for a performance in the gymnasium "Sokolovna," in the fall of 1944, by the conductor, Karel Schächter, and the stage director, Karl Meinhard, who came to Terezín from Berlin. However, the premiere never took place there, because in the big transports to Auschwitz in October 1944, Ullmann and most of the involved artists went to meet their death. The score of the opera and Ullmann's other compositions written in Terezín had been considered lost, and only much later they were found in London in the possession of Dr. H. G. Adler.[18]

The activities of Franz Eugen Klein as conductor of operas and piano accompanist in Terezín are well documented. Very little is known, however, about the man himself, and almost nothing about his work as composer. Franz Eugen Klein (born April 29, 1912) came to Terezín with his wife, Susanne, in October 1942. While still in the concentration camp, he produced a major work, the opera *Der gläserne Berg* (*The Glass Mountain*). The only musical memento of this work is an autographed souvenir of his sojourn in Terezín, written by the composer for the collector Karl Herrmann,[19] which quotes the main motive of the opera in the piano reduction. It also indicates

---

[18]*Der Kaiser von Atlantis* was finally premiered in December 1975 in Amsterdam under the baton of Kerry Woodward, who edited the original score. The libretto was translated into English by Aaron Kramer.

[19]After the war he changed his name to Karel Heřman.

that the opera was composed between November 1943 and January 24, 1944. According to Bedřich Borges, one of the main participants, the opera was prepared and performed once for the Council of Elders in Terezín. It did not obtain the permit for public performances in the ghetto. The actual reasons are not known.

Borges described the opera as too modernistic, in style similar to that of Alban Berg, but most probably of inferior quality. In his opinion, that was also the reason why it never reached the public. The score perished, and it is very doubtful that it will ever be found. Even the content of the libretto and its author are not known, and the work will most probably remain an enigma for posterity. It is equally unknown whether Klein wrote any other compositions in Terezín. He left for Auschwitz with the transport Er 944 on October 16, 1944. During the selection, he asked the infamous Dr. Mengele to let him follow a bespectacled friend, unaware that this request would lead him into the gas chamber. Mengele gladly obliged.

FIVE

Chamber Music
and Recitals

While the first musical efforts in Terezín were undertaking their first painful steps, caused by the absence of suitable facilities and appropriate accompanying instruments, the field of chamber music enjoyed the most favorable conditions. The members of the Council of Elders lived separately in their own rooms, and they could bring from home some of their luxurious belongings. Since several of these men had a strong affinity for serious music, it is no wonder that musical instruments and equipment headed their list of priorities. Thus, Otto Zucker, an ardent amateur violinist, brought not only his violin but also a phonograph with a large record collection. Dr. Erich Klapp came with his cello, and Dr. Paul Eppstein, who came to Terezín in January 1943 as a new head of the Council, had his beautiful grand piano shipped to the ghetto all the way from Berlin.

From the beginning of 1942, these people initiated musical soirées in their living quarters, and they invited the best available musicians as well as listeners from the ranks of internees. The first one to be called upon was the well known violinist Egon Ledeč, who from 1926 until the German occupation served as associate concertmaster of the prestigious Czech Philharmonic in Prague. Born in Kostelec nad Orlicí (Bohemia) on March 16, 1889, he studied violin at the Prague Conservatory with the famous teacher Otakar Ševčík, among others, and was active as soloist and chamber music player. Together with Dr. Ilona Král, the violist Viktor Kohn, and Dr. Klapp, they formed in the ghetto the first string quartet, the so-called "Doctors' Quartet." In Dr. Klapp's apartment each week they performed quartets of Haydn, Beethoven, and Dvořák. The formation of other groups followed, and soon there were string ensembles from trios to sextets in existence.

However, the oldest claim to chamber music comes from Arnošt Weiss, although under quite unexpected circumstances. As he recalls in his memoirs, Weiss came to Terezín on January 30, 1942, and on the next day he was assigned with twenty-five other men to the "Cavalier" barracks. It was then, as he was standing in a latrine and whistling a tune, that an elderly man approached him with a question:

"Look, young man, do you know what you are whistling?"
"Certainly," Weiss replied. "Beethoven's Razoumovsky Quartet No. 1."

After that, the man introduced himself as a former member of the Berlin Philharmonic and later concertmaster of the Opera in Ústí nad Labem (Bohemia), Mr. Freudenthal. Still in the latrine, he took over whistling the first violin part, and Weiss filled in expertly the three remaining voices.

The weekly meetings of the "Doctors' Quartet," which actually had its origins back in Prague, were informal sight-readings of the chamber music literature, and, although guests had been invited, these were not polished presentations. Egon Ledeč later formed his own Ledeč Quartet together with a second violinist, an amateur by the name of Schneider, Viktor Kohn on the viola, and his brother, Paul Kohn, on the cello. After the arrival of the transport from Vienna in August 1942, the elderly former member of the famous Rosé Quartet, Julius Stwertka, took up the position of second violinist. In 1942, most of these musical events took place in the

"Magdeburg" barracks, and only later the Ledeč Quartet performed openly under the auspices of the *Freizeitgestaltung*. Finally, in the summer of 1944, Ledeč presented a brand new ensemble, in which his collaborators were Messrs. Viktor Kohn, violinist Adolf Kraus, and cellist Dauber. This formation was hailed by Viktor Ullmann: "by all means a gain for our chamber music," after their first public appearance, in which they played a string quartet by Haydn, *Divertimento Ebraico* of Siegmund Schul, and Borodin's ever popular *Quartet in D Minor*. Unfortunately, this collaboration did not last very long, because on October 17 of the same year Egon Ledeč perished in Auschwitz.

An ensemble with higher artistic aspirations was the so-called Terezín Quartet (*Theresienstadt Streichquartett*), composed of four young musicians, violinists Karel Fröhlich and Heinrich "Bubbi" Taussig, violist Romuald Süssmann, and cellist Friedrich Mark. They had already started playing together in Prague and had participated frequently in private Jewish recitals. After their arrival in Terezín they renewed their musical activities in a serious professional manner. Instead of merely playing or sight-reading the quartet literature, they studied their parts in detail, and under Fröhlich's leadership wrote uniform bowings and with utmost care worked on dynamics and all around interpretation. Very often, Gideon Klein or Karel Ančerl would attend their rehearsals with a score in his hand and advise them on finer points which would otherwise elude them. There was no shortage of unsolicited advice by kibitzers who liked to listen during their practice. Fröhlich and his colleagues had a long-term plan to perform not only in Terezín, but to continue after the liberation with their mutual career. Because of this, the repertoire of the Terezín Quartet was rather limited: Beethoven's *Quartet in C Minor, opus 18*, Brahms' *B-flat Major*, Mozart's *D Major*, Josef Suk's *Meditation on an Ancient Czech Chorale*, Tchaikovsky's *Andante Cantabile*, and two original compositions written in Terezín, *Variations on His Own Theme* by Hans Krása and *Praeludium and Fugue* by Gideon Klein.

The leader of the group, Karel Fröhlich, was a native of Olomouc in Moravia (born November 20, 1917). After finishing his Liberal Arts and private violin studies there, he entered the Prague

Conservatory and then the Master School, where he became a pupil of Professor Jindřich Feld in 1940. As a very talented young artist, he gave several solo recitals in 1940 and 1941, under an assumed name, since any public appearances by Jews were strictly prohibited. In 1941 he was sent for a short stay at a labor camp in Lípa, and not too long after his return home, his deportation to Terezín followed. While Süssmann remained in the ghetto until the end of the war, the other three went to Auschwitz in October 1944, and only Fröhlich was lucky enough to survive the ordeal.

Karel Fröhlich's interest in chamber music prompted him into collaboration with other artists in various ensembles. Eleven times he played the piano quartets of Brahms and Dvořák with the pianist Gideon Klein and his string quartet colleagues Süssmann and Mark. On April 17, 1944, he performed Mozart's *Piano Quartet in G Minor* with the pianist Juliette Arányi and Messrs. Snyders and Swab. In various combinations with the same artists he played in piano trios, string tercets as a violist, and, of course, in many recitals.

Likewise, Fröhlich's associates took part in performances of various groups. The aforementioned *Piano Quartet in G Minor* by Mozart received a favorable review from Viktor Ullmann; however, the performers were Arányi, Süssmann, and Mark, and the very young Pavel Kling played the violin part. Noteworthy is the fact that all four artists played without music. As Kling recalls it, this was the result of a bet between him and the violinist Taussig, the prize being a can of liver paté.

Gideon Klein soon established himself as one of the moving spirits on the Terezín musical scene, thanks to his extraordinary talent and wide education. It is, therefore, not surprising that after the performance of Beethoven's *Trio*, Op. 70, No. 2, and Brahms' *Trio*, Op. 8, with Kling and Mark, Viktor Ullmann appraised their effort in the following words:

> The performance is noteworthy for its excellent preparation, done by Gideon Klein, who himself mastered the difficult piano part with élan and reliable feeling for the style. Paul (Pavel) Kling made his debut on the violin with a lot of success, and he is on the way up and

very talented, Friedrich Mark has already proven himself often as a splendid chamber music player.

Equally, Heinrich Taussig ventured from the second violin of Fröhlich's group to the piano trio with the cellist Paul Kohn and the pianist Wolfgang (Wolfi) Lederer. In March 1944 they premiered a program comprising Beethoven's *Trio in D major*, "Ghost," and *Trio in G minor*, Op. 1, a graduation work of the Czech composer Vítězslav Novák. The very good impression from their first public appearance, followed by no less than ten repeats, evoked considerable expectations and hope for the future, but in Terezín life itself was very uncertain, and Lederer became the only survivor of this ensemble.

At times, even larger groups performed chamber music. On one such occasion, Taussig, Kling, Süssmann, and Mark were joined by Paul Kohn on second cello and Karel Ančerl on second viola in the presentation of Schubert's *Quintet in G Major*, Op. 163, and Brahms' *Sextet in G Major*, Op. 36.

Frequent changes in personnel were increased also by incidental absence of the regular members due to any kind of indisposition. Thus it was a great privilege for the young Pavel Kling to sit at the second desk of Fröhlich's professional quartet, or for the amateur Arnošt Weiss to help out in the same function in the ensemble of Egon Ledeč.

One of the special problems in playing chamber music was the lack of musical material. Some scores were made available through the courtesy of the members of the Council of Elders, some were brought illegally by the inmates, and some found their way into Terezín as the need arose. Arnošt Weiss proved to be, in this respect, a valuable asset. As head of a construction section, on rare occasions he had to go out of the ghetto on official business. This way, he came across an establishment manufacturing woodwind instruments; its proprietor, Mr. Žalud, was a trustworthy man, ready to help. Weiss explained to him the situation in the ghetto and handed him a list of needed compositions. Shortly after, he proudly delivered quartets

Kammermusik-Abend.

FRANZ SCHUBERT:
QUINTETT C-DUR OP. 163

JOHANNES BRAHMS:
SEXTETT G-DUR OP. 36

AUSFÜHRENDE:

I. Violine: Heinrich G. Taussig
II. Violine: Paul Klink
I. Viola: Romuald Süssmann
II. Viola: Karel Ančerl
Violoncelli: Friedrich Mark
Paul Kohn

Program of a chamber music recital.

of Beethoven, Mozart, Schubert, and Dvořák to the hands of the eagerly waiting musicians.

The solo recitals could not fare very well for a while, because there was no suitable accompanying instrument in an appropriate hall or room. The modest singing of songs and even arias without accompaniment and solo violin playing in attics and basements extended well into 1942. Although not as effective as regular recitals, these performances nevertheless fulfilled their mission: to bring a little sunshine into the otherwise somber and grey life of the prisoners. But even so, real artistic offerings had been presented when, for example, Karel Fröhlich played movements from Bach's sonatas and partitas for violin solo in the Terezín barracks. Unlikely instruments such as the accordion were transformed in the hands of Wolfgang Lederer as almost a perfect match for Fröhlich's violin, not only in the accompaniment of some short pieces but even in an entire concerto by Mozart. Here also, Necessity was the mother of Invention.

The first improvement came with the discovery of a decrepit piano. Although without legs, it could be put into such condition that it could be used for the accompaniment of vocal rehearsals and for piano recitals as well. As the demand for the use of the piano grew stronger, several pianos together with some smaller instruments and sheet music were delivered to the ghetto from Prague, thanks to the intervention of the officers of the *Freizeitgestaltung*. Since this organization administered all kinds of cultural and even sports activities, it was able to enrich Terezín with a large book collection and other equipment, otherwise not available to the inmates.

Once the pianos were delivered to the ghetto, the pianists were assigned time for practicing and performing, and from that instant the musical and cultural life mushroomed to such an extent that every day several concurrent musical and theatrical performances took place, besides the lectures, debates, and sports activities. Several outstanding pianists emerged shortly in recitals, some of them not to be forgotten in a lifetime. The first place went without doubt to Professor Bernard Kaff from Brno. Native of that Moravian capital, born on May 14, 1905, Kaff studied piano at the branch of the Prague Master School there and later in Vienna and Berlin. On his concert tours in Czechoslovakia, Germany, Austria, France, Yugoslavia, and the Netherlands, he often introduced contemporary piano compositions, many of them dedicated to him. At the same time, he found enough time to teach in Brno and Vienna for eleven

Bernard Kaff. Drawing by Petr Kien.

years, from 1925 to 1936, and in the last few years before his incarceration in Terezín, exclusively in Brno.

It was Bernard Kaff who apparently gave the first piano recital on the instrument found in Terezín. No matter how dilapidated the piano was, under his fingers it came alive with exquisite sound. As with most of the performances in Terezín, the number of Kaff's recitals is uncertain, since the majority of programs were repeated. The preserved documents indicate four complete programs, two of them dedicated to works of Beethoven, one to Chopin and Liszt, and one comprised of works of various composers, including one by Kaff's colleague, Pavel Haas. A review by Viktor Ullmann, that severe but knowledgeable Terezín critic, speaks enthusiastically of still another program, in which Kaff premiered Haas *Partita in Old Style*, especially written for him, together with the cycle, *In the Mist*, by Leoš Janáček, and *Pictures at an Exhibition* by Modest Mussorgsky. This recital was held later on June 28, 1944, and of that performance Ullmann had this to say:

> Kaff played the Partita with verve and mastery. This time, he actually chose an ascetic program. Janáček's *In the Mist* remains, at any rate, a thankless work for a pianist. . . . Who does not think here of the speaking voice of the Moravian peasants in Janáček's operas? It was transferred to the piano with unheard audacity.
>
> Mussorgsky, the progenitor of Impressionism, is the second operatic composer, whom Kaff introduced as a Master of the piano, ingeniously in contrast with the first one. And one does not miss Ravel's orchestration of the *Pictures at an Exhibition*, when Kaff plays them, raised above the technique, colorful, bizarre, and always molding the necessary and never the arbitrary. Art is based on ability and necessity. Kaff does not use any willfulness, he plays in the spirit of the composer and yet with inspiration and individuality.

Besides its high artistic quality, the performance of Mussorgsky's *Pictures* had an enormous political significance, although it is not known whether Kaff introduced the piece for that purpose. As previously said, the first performance took place in June of 1944—in other words, at the time of the German retreat on all fronts, especially the Russian. Since the Czech Jews were generally oriented to the socialist left, it is not surprising that the majestic "Grand Gate of Kiev" (the last section of the Mussorgsky's composition) represented to the prisoners the final liberation by the Russian armies.

The only time Professor Kaff teamed up with another artist was in the sonata recital with Karel Fröhlich. Only two musicians of such magnitude could do justice to two monumental works: Beethoven's *Kreutzer Sonata* and *Sonata in A Major* by César Franck. Kaff did not accompany any recitals in Terezín; nevertheless he did not hesitate to share his talent and knowledge in debates and even formal instruction of the young novices in the realm of musical arts.

There were in the ghetto no fewer than half a dozen concert pianists who performed frequently in solo recitals and numerous other presentations. Gideon Klein offered two piano recitals with works of Mozart, Beethoven, and Schumann; and Janáček, Suk, Brahms, and Bach, with six and nine repeats respectively. Reviewing the second program, Ullmann came to the ensuing conclusion:

> Gideon Klein is, without doubt, a very remarkable talent. His is the cool, matter-of-fact style of the new youth; one has to marvel at his strangely early stylistic maturity. The pioneers of 1770, the champions of the then *ars nova*, were adherents of *Sturm und Drang*.[20] Our youth has strong, intelligent brains; let us hope that the heart will be able to lift itself into the head.

Unlike Kaff, Klein and most of the other pianists became involved in chamber music, recital accompaniments, operas, oratorios, or other genres.

One of the busiest pianists in Terezín was Edith Steiner-Kraus. Her first musical experience there was a joint piano recital in the schoolhouse. Three participating pianists, Bernard Kaff, Gideon Klein, and Truda Reisová, shared the program, each playing one sonata by Beethoven. The instrument was, at that time, the only one

---

[20]*Sturm und Drang* (Storm and Stress) was a literary movement of the latter part of the 18th century.

in Terezín, standing on crates, and it had to be serviced between the numbers by the piano tuner, Mr. Pick. Edith Steiner-Kraus had to work in a mica factory, where she sat next to her very good friend and colleague, Alice Herz-Sommer. They worked rather slowly, often while singing folk songs. Both of them received permission to practice the piano one hour a day, and in the evening they could perform in recitals. And it was that battered old piano which very possibly saved the life of Edith Steiner-Kraus. Not too long after her arrival in Terezín, her name appeared on the list of a transport to Auschwitz. When somebody suggested to her that she might evade this dangerous duty by giving a recital, she did not let such an opportunity pass. Although sheet music was not at her disposal, Edith had enough pieces memorized for a full recital. By that time, the legless piano had been transported to the "Magdeburg" barracks. The program consisted of Bach's *Toccata and Fugue in D Major*, Mozart's *Sonnata in B-flat Major*, five *Intermezzi and Capricii* by Brahms, Chopin's *Nocturne and Ballade*, and two concert polkas by Smetana. The successful recital was scheduled for a repeat performance when an inmate escaped from Terezín. For punishment, all cultural activities were canceled from October 27 until November 2; nevertheless, Edith Steiner-Kraus reached her main objective and remained in Terezín for the duration of the war. Her pianistic activities progressed at an ever accelerated tempo.

One of the concert grand pianos brought into Terezín from Prague was placed in the city hall, which thus became one of the formal gathering places. At that time, the practice period for the pianists was increased to two hours daily. Edith Steiner-Kraus played her all-Bach recital there about ten times. In an evening of music by Franz Schubert, she performed two of his sonatas, and between them Karel Berman and Marion Podolier sang several of his songs. Besides the Old Masters, other programs included compositions of Ullmann and Haas, music from the rococo era—especially noteworthy for the performance of Haydn's *Oboe Concerto* in the interpretation of Professor Armin Tiroler from Vienna (born 1873, died in Auschwitz, 1944)—and numerous special solo presentations for youngsters, old people, even in the Cafe. Equally frequent were Edith Steiner-Kraus' appearances with other artists,

Edith Steiner-Kraus. Drawing by an unknown artist.

such as recitals of four-hand piano music with the Dutch pianist Beatrice Pimentel, concertos with the accompaniment of a second piano played by Elsa Schiller from Berlin, evenings of sonatas with the Dutch violinist Tromp, playing as accompanist to singers, or in collaboration with the so-called entertainment orchestra, led by the Danish conductor Peter Deutsch. Edith Steiner-Kraus escaped the fate of the majority of her peers once more in September of 1944, when her husband was sent to Auschwitz. She was ready to join him voluntarily in the transport, but she heeded to the advice of the Council Depty, Otto Zucker, and remained in the ghetto, never to see her husband again.

It is difficult to say which one of the musicians was most in demand in Terezín. The pianist Alice Herz-Sommer came there somewhat later, in July 1943, with the last transport from Prague, because her husband worked for the Jewish Community as transport despatcher. However, she still managed to appear on the Terezín podia more than one hundred times. In her five different solo recitals she performed sonatas by Beethoven, compositions by Schumann, Brahms, Smetana, Debussy, Viktor Ullmann, and later twenty-four études of Frédéric Chopin in one evening. Of course, all of these programs had to be repeated many times. Viktor Ullmann, in one of his reviews, called her "the friend of Beethoven, Schumann, and Chopin," and he expressed words of thanks on behalf of the Terezín audiences for "many delightful hours." Indeed, Beethoven was one of her favorite composers. She proved that through a number of recitals in which she played his sonatas for piano and violin with several partners, Egon Ledeč, Professor Hermann Leydensdorff[21] from the Netherlands, and her own brother, Pavel Herz. This affinity sprang doubtless from her studies with the great Beethoven interpreter, Conrad Ansorge, while her interest in modern music—performances of works by Ullmann, Haas, etc.— had its roots in her association with her teachers, Eduard Steuermann, a pupil of Schoenberg, and the Czech pianist Václav Štěpán.

Several additional pianists enriched the Terezín musical life. Among them Renée Gärtner-Geiringer took a very prominent

[21]In all documents from Terezín, the name of Prof. Hessel Hermann Leydensdorff is spelled incorrectly as Hermann Leidensdorf.

place. This Viennese artist (born March 9, 1908) came to Terezín in October 1942. By the time she left for her death in Auschwitz gas chambers two years later, in October 1944, she had presented at least four different programs in no less than thirty-two repeats. Her repertoire included sonatas of Beethoven, Brahms, and Haydn, as well as compositions by Bach, Schumann, Schubert, Chopin, Liszt, and Franck. Although Viktor Ullmann considered her more as a cembalo virtuoso, nevertheless, in his review of her most successful program, performed a total of twelve times, he paid her this compliment: "Mrs. Gärtner-Geiringer, this versatile and excellent musician, is equipped with a virtuoso technique of the genuine Viennese school. . . . From less frequently played works, we heard in exemplary interpretation the 'Prelude, Chorale and Fugue' of César Franck." Like the majority of pianists, Renée Gärtner-Geiringer was a sought-after piano accompanist.

In direct contrast to the very busy performers, Juliette Arányi, a piano virtuoso from Slovakia (born 1912), very seldom played in Terezín. There is only one extant program of her recital in the ghetto with compositions by Bach, Mozart, Debussy, and Chopin, and the previously mentioned involvement in the Brahms' piano quartet. This is even more surprising when one considers that this artist had appeared on the concert stages since she was six years old, and enjoyed such a reputation that in 1940 Viktor Ullmann wrote for her a piano concerto and his *Third Piano Sonata*. Arányi's life came to an untimely end in Auschwitz, in the fall of 1944.

One of the basic problems facing the musicians in the ghetto was the lack of musical material. In this respect the pianists had an advantage, because they could perform alone. Since all of them had a distinguished solo career prior to their arrival to Terezín, they had a substantial repertoire memorized and therefore were able to reach into this reserve and present complete works in the original version to their audiences. What hampered their early efforts was, at first, the total absence of a piano, and then the use of the "relic" found in the gymnasium. Only later the situation improved, and everybody took full advantage of the new conditions.

The first recitals by other instrumentalists and vocalists were presented without any accompaniment or with an accordion.

Although this was not an ideal instrument, especially for classical music, it had to suffice, and in the hands of a proficient musician it could almost perform miracles. The subsequent find of a harmonium further enhanced the musical possibilities, and, once the pianos were available, there was no limit to the artistic expression.

The man with the most formidable artistic achievements in Terezín was Karel Fröhlich. His involvement in chamber music was described earlier, and so were his performances with the accordionist Kurt Maier. Fröhlich's later collaboration with Wolfgang Lederer, playing the harmonium, resulted in an almost unbelievable program—certainly for a concentration camp—in which he performed the *Violin Concerto in D Minor* by Giuseppe Tartini; *Sonata in G Minor* for violin solo by J. S. Bach; the entire *Violin Concerto in A Minor* of Antonín Dvořák; *Caprice* No. 13 for violin solo by Niccolò Paganini; *Chanson Palestinienne* of Paul Kirman; and the virtuoso showpiece, the *Zigeunerweisen* of Pablo de Sarasate.

In a signed statement of his concert activities in Terezín, dated May 20, 1944, Fröhlich lists compositions performed by him up to that day, and also his plans for his upcoming recitals. The seemingly endless list contains the concertos by Vivaldi (A Minor), Bach (E Major), Mozart (D Major), and Tartini and Dvořák; sonatas for violin and piano by Leclair (D Major), Tartini (B-flat Major), Mozart (E Minor), Franck (A Major), Beethoven ("Kreutzer"), and sonatina by Dvořák; one complete sonata for violin solo by J.S. Bach and several excerpts from others; and various compositions by Paganini (including the extremely difficult "Witches' Dance"), Sarasate, Saint-Saëns, Brahms, Schubert, Smetana, arrangements by Fritz Kreisler, and several more. Then, a mere week later, on May 27, Fröhlich appeared in a sonata recital with Professor Ferencz Weiss, formerly of the Liszt Academy in Budapest and a long time resident of the Netherlands, where he was active as a teacher. Once again, it was Viktor Ullmann who expressed his opinion about this recital:

> At any rate, Karel Fröhlich brought a beautiful and well chosen program besides Bach's transparent and playful *Sonata in A Major*, two stars of the first magnitude of the violin literature: Brahms' *Sonata in G Major* and Beethoven's seventh in C Minor. Fröhlich is a violinist of

Karel Fröhlich. Drawing by Petr Kien.

V I O L I N K O N Z E R T

Karl F r ö h l i c h (Violine)
Wolfgang L e d e r e r (Harmonium)

GIUSEPPE TARTINI	Violinkonzert d – moll Allegro–Grave–Presto
JOHANN SEBASTIAN BACH	Sonate g–moll für Solo violine Adagio – Fuga – Sizilia Presto

— . — . — . — . — . — . — . — . — . — . —

ANTONÍN DVOŘÁK	Violinkonzert a – moll Allegro ma non troppo Adagio ma non troppo Allegro giocoso , ma n troppo
NICOLO PAGANINI	Caprice Nr. 13 für Solo voline (Der lachende Faun)
PAUL KIRMAN	Chanson Palestinienne (Alte hebräische Weiser
PABLO de SARASATE	Zigeunerweisen

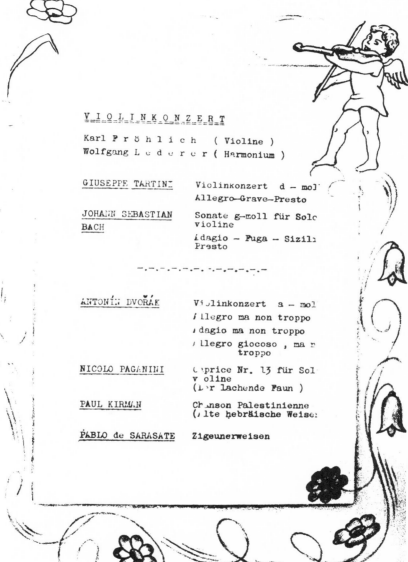

Program of a violin recital of Karel Fröhlich.

stature, without doubt an outstanding talent and on the best way of development. Where this will lead him yet or what it will withhold from him, with the best intentions cannot be foreseen, of course. In any case, he has strong and fine abilities and already today is capable of shaping. . . . He was accompanied on the piano by Ferencz Weiss, who is a really excellent pianist, but who can be praised only for his technical ability.

At the time of his departure for Auschwitz, Fröhlich was working or contemplating work on the entire violin repertoire, which included all the great concertos of Beethoven, Brahms, Tchaikovsky, Mendelssohn, Paganini, Wieniawski; the complete cycle of Beethoven's sonatas, Bach's sonatas and partitas for violin solo, Paganini's Caprices, as well as a number of virtuoso compositions. He was also considering formation of a new string quartet with Messrs. Geissmar, Snyders, and Swab. Luckily, in Fröhlich's case, his plans were merely interrupted by his stay in Auschwitz, and he resumed his musical activities after the war, though not realizing all his original intentions.

Karel Fröhlich had a unique position in Terezín. Still young, he was already a very mature artist. His only potential competitor was Egon Ledeč, who, instead, supported Fröhlich's endeavors and graciously gave his much younger colleague the chance to get more experience and exposure. There were several younger aspiring violinists, such as Pavel Kling or Tomáš Mandl, but these held the young master in high esteem and, as the situation permitted, studied with him. Occasionally these and other violinists, such as Adolf Schächter, the brother of the conductor, performed in solo or joint recitals, and sometimes other instrumentalists also mounted the Terezín podia.

The enormous quantity of talent among singers in the ghetto could not be satisfied in operatic performances only, so most of them appeared in numerous recitals of lieder, songs, and operatic excerpts. Preserved programs document the recitals of the excellent Dutch tenor Machiel Gobets,[22] accompanied by Rafael Schächter

---

[22]Also spelled as Michael or Michel Gobetz.

and Renée Gärtner-Geiringer, in which he performed lieder and arias by Schubert, Brahms, Handel, Donizetti, Verdi, Puccini, and some less known composers, and even several Yiddish folk songs. David Grünfeld chose for one of his recitals Italian songs and arias, and Walter Windholz, a basso from the Brno Opera, presented a special recital for the opening of the new concert hall in the City Hall in June 1943. The first half was devoted to lieder of Old Masters, Shubert, Brahms, and Smetana, while the second featured the Jewish composers, Gustav Mahler (*Lieder eines fahrenden Gesellen*), and the Terezín inmates, Viktor Ullmann and Hans Krása. Additional noteworthy solo recitals were given by Karel Berman, Hedda Grab-Kernmayr, and Fritz Königsgarten, a talented tenor from Brno.

The concerts of solely operatic music were directed, not surprisingly, by the Viennese conductor Franz Eugen Klein, who accompanied the singers on the piano in the most famous arias and duets from the international repertoire. Once in a while he would add variety with a rendition of a less known operatic excerpt, such as an aria from the opera *Der Evangelimanm* by the Austrian composer Wilhelm Kienzl with the soloist Magda Spiegel, formerly from the opera in Frankfurt. The field of operatic music of Czech composers, Smetana, Dvořák, and Blodek, was aptly served by Karel Berman.

The bulk of the musical offerings included a variety of artists in diversified programs of works by different composers. However, sometimes the entire evening featured music of one single Master. Beethoven was, of course, the most likely candidate for such an honor. In comparison, an evening of lieder by Gustav Mahler was rather extraordinary. It took place on July 9, 1943, when the mezzo soprano Hilde Aronson-Lindt and the baritone Walter Windholz, accompanied on the piano by Dr. Otto König, sang selections from *Des Knaben Wunderhorn, Kindertotenlieder,* and *Lieder eines fahrenden Gesellen.*

The versatile Viktor Ullmann founded and directed the *Studio für neue Musik* (Studio for New Music). There is no evidence how many programs he actually presented and when, but two remaining posters disclose extraordinary imagination. The second program dealt exclusively with works of young composers from Terezín— Gideon Klein, Karel Berman, Siegmund Schul, and Heinz Alt—

David Grünfeld.

Program of a recital of Walter Windholz.

Studio für neue Musik

Leitung: Viktor Ullmann

2. Konzert

Junge Autoren in Theresienstadt

1. **Gideon Klein:**
   Die Pest, + Lieder für Altstime
   u. Klavier;   Dichtung: Peter Kien

2. **Heinz Alt:**
   6 Miniaturen   für Klavier

3. **Siegmund Schul:**
   2 Chassidische Tänze für Violine u. Cello

4. **Karl Bermann:**
   Ponpata

5. **Siegmund Schul:**
   Diverti-Mento Ebraico für Streichquartett

Mitwirkende:

aronson-Lind, Kling, Ledeč-Quartett
Dr. Reiner; R.-Schächter; Weissenstein

Program of the "Studio for New Music,"
featuring works of young Terezín composers.

Program of the "Studio for New Music."

Program poster of the "Music of the Rococo."

while the fourth program combined piano compositions and lieder of Arnold Schoenberg, Max Reger, Gustav Mahler, and the Czech avant-gardist Alois Hába, with virtually unknown works of the great conductors Bruno Walter and Alexander Zemlinsky.

Notable attention was paid to old music as well, and once again the tireless Viktor Ullmann was the moving spirit behind this endeavor. In several concerts of the Collegium Musicum, he was responsible for the artistic direction and even found time to prepare himself as one of the participating pianists. In a very similar program of the previously mentioned concert of "Music of the Rococo," the alto Ada Schwarz-Klein, the venerable Professor Armin Tiroler, violinist Adolf Kraus, and cellist Paul Kohn, accompanied by Edith Steiner-Kraus, presented works of Boccherini, Tartini, Pergolesi, Paisiello, Rolle, and Haydn.

Upon a closer scrutiny of the existing programs from Terezín, one cannot help but detect the ostentatious absence of the name of Richard Wagner. Even when one takes into consideration his demands on the performer, the primary reason lies in the fact that this composer embodied the German megalomania and was chosen as obvious artistic representative of the Nazi regime and a favorite of Adolf Hitler.

To a reader who is aware of the actual meaning of the term "concentration camp," the scope and frequency of the cultural activities seem totally unbelievable, especially if one realizes that the musical activities represented only a part of a broader cultural life, which included theatrical presentations, lectures on a great variety of subjects, recitation of poetry, and to a certain degree also sports activities. A concentration camp is a place of detention where people are imprisoned; however, they do not spend time in small cells behind bars. Most concentration camps are comprised of barracks, surrounded usually by electrified barbed wire fence. In the case of Terezín, the Nazis used a conveniently located town with ramparts serving the same objective. The inmates had to work in assigned details, which included running the camp itself. During free time they had a certain amount of freedom of movement and activities within the confines of the town. In Terezín, the situation was even more favorable, because the ghetto was administered by the Jewish

Council of Elders, who were able to negotiate sizable concessions from the Nazis. Thus the establishment of the *Freizeitgestaltung* not only allowed the cultural activities in themselves, but its branched-out structure could protect a relatively large number of people by employing them as performers, lecturers, and administrators, rather than as laborers elsewhere. Ultimately, this led to gross Nazi exploitation, in which Terezín was used as a model ghetto for propaganda purposes; the Nazis not only permitted, but directly ordered many of these activities in connection with the visits of the International Red Cross Committee. On the other hand, the prisoners welcomed any occasion to find surcease, for at least a fleeting moment, from the grim realities of everyday life.

SIX

Orchestras in Terezín

The abundance of musical in-
struments in Terezín incited Karel Ančerl to form a string orchestra.
This happened, naturally, only when the *Freizeitgestaltung* was
already in effect, since any activity of this size would have been very
difficult to conceal. There was also the problem of larger instruments,
cellos and a double bass, which had to be delivered into the ghetto,
with the help of the administration, from Prague.

By the time Karel Ančerl came to Terezín, he had behind him a
distinguished career. He was born in the Bohemian town of Tučapy
on April 11, 1908 and received his education in Prague, first at a
gymnasium, and then at he Conservatory of Music, where he
majored in conducting and composition. In the decade between his
graduation in 1929 and the German occupation, Ančerl assisted
Hermann Scherchen as a vocal coach in the Munich Opera House,
conducted the orchestra in the Liberated Theater (*Osvobozené
divadlo*) in Prague; from 1933 to 1938 he worked as sound engineer
and conductor at the State Radio in Prague. In the years 1933–34 he
attended the conducting department of the Master School in Prague
as a student of Professor Václav Talich, the "Toscanini of the Slavic
world." Finally, the years 1942 to 1944 marked his stay in Terezín
and his musical involvement there.

Karel Ančerl. Drawing by Petr Kien.

The string orchestra, assembled in the ghetto by Ančerl, had a respectable size: sixteen first violins, twelve seconds, eight violas, six cellos, and one double bass. All of its members were men with a single exception: a strikingly attractive blonde, playing the lonely bass. To solve the balance problem caused by the insufficient number of the lowest instruments, Ančerl asked some of the cellists to double the bass line. The high quality of the ensemble was virtually guaranteed by the fact that many of the players came from the professional ranks of several European countries. The young Karel Fröhlich offered the concertmaster's chair to the experienced Egon Ledeč, but the latter graciously declined and took the second spot—as in the Czech Philharmonic—thus giving Fröhlich the chance to become a concertmaster. The orchestra was truly international, having, besides the larger contingent of Czech musicians, players from Germany, Denmark, and even several former members of the world famous Amsterdam Concertgebouw Orchestra.

Ančerl prepared two different programs with the ensemble. The first consisted of Handel's *Concerto Grosso in F Major*, Mozart's *Eine kleine Nachtmusik*, and Bach's *Violin Concerto in E Major*, with Fröhlich as soloist. The number of repeats is questionable, depending on the sources, but an educated guess puts it above a dozen performances. Sometimes the soloists alternated, and, instead of Fröhlich, the handsome Gideon Klein played the solo part in Bach's *Piano Concerto in D Minor*, to the delight of countless hopelessly enamored, admiring young ladies. The second program featured only Czech music. It included the *Meditation on an Ancient Czech Chorale* by Josef Suk, the *Serenade for Strings* of Antonín Dvořák, and a composition especially written in Terezín by Pavel Haas, the *Study for Strings*. Unlike the former, this program was presented only twice, in the late summer of 1944, on a concert stage, erected on the Terezín square, in connection with one of the visits of the International Red Cross Committee. This was all a part of a much larger project, a fraudulent propaganda film about the "idyllic" life of the Jews in the ghetto, in which one of these performances has been immortalized. The actual concert presentation look place in a concert hall on September 13, 1944, and received this favorable review from Viktor Ullmann:

Concert stage on the Terezín square.

Karel Ančerl is a conductor of caliber and impressive know-how. It is a proof of his qualities and also his superhuman patience that in heroic labor he welded together and brought up this musical body. As a conductor, Ančerl reminds one of Talich and Hermann Scherchen; like the latter, he was and is a pioneer of new music as well, and so he succeeded in presenting a very beautiful and inspiring premiere: Pavel Haas' *Study for a String Orchestra*.

A masterly, polyrhytmically interesting introduction leads to an ingenious, energetic fugue–exposition, whose marked theme with its hiatus becomes easy to remember, and lets rise a svelte fugato, followed by a lively, folkloristically flavored scherzando; after a resting point, which takes the place of a slow movement—in fact, we even recognized two themes—there follows an abbreviated reprise of the fugato and a thrilling, motoric coda as a finale. The *Study* emerges entirely from the idiomatic character of the string orchestra, and sounds good; it is less revolutionary than Haas' works written here previously. Altogether, there is an apparent hand of the musician who knows what he wants and also is capable of doing it. The accomplishment of the orchestra—except for the lack of double basses—was satisfactory throughout. Haas, Ančerl, and his orchestra were gratefully acclaimed.

Suk's *Meditation* (*on an Ancient Chorale*) finds a new, original, epic chorale arrangement. It is a deeply earnest piece, rising up to passionate ecstasy, and it unfolds powers of the string orchestra, not disavowing the characteristic harmony and melody of a great neo-Romantic.

Antonín Dvořák's famous *Serenade* took, as always, the hearts of the listeners by storm. It is a splendid specimen of a musical genius, as Dvořák is, altogether, one of the few masters with a continuous flow of an inexhaustible wealth of strong, brilliant ideas . . . besides him this is characteristic only of Bach, Mozart, and Schubert. The technically easier and joyful work suits our orchestra, and in its rendition was at its best.

(Signed) Viktor Ullmann

On April 30, 1944, a new concert recreation hall was opened on West Street. It was such a formal affair that the public needed reserved tickets for admittance. The gala program presented on that occasion consisted of several musical numbers, recitation of Czech poetry, and a speech by the chairman of the Council of Elders. For the first selection, Karel Ančerl chose the theme from Beethoven's Ninth Symphony. The string orchestra had been enlarged by several wind and brass instruments, and Rafael Schächter filled in the remaining missing parts on the piano. At the conclusion of the program, the orchestra played the *Serenade for Strings* of Antonín Dvořák.

The somewhat limited repertoire of the ensemble can be explained by the fact that not all members worked for the *Freizeitgestaltung*, and thus could rehearse only during their free time after work. Even the conductor, Karel Ančerl, was only a part-time musician in Terezín, having a full-time job as a kitchen helper. Furthermore, the orchestra was augmented by some inexperienced, even though excellent, young players and a few amateurs.

The string orchestra flourished until October 1944, when most of the musicians and their leader set out on what happened to be for many of them their last journey to Auschwitz.

It may seem almost unbelievable, but Ančerl's orchestra was not the only one in Terezín. Far from that: there were at least four concert orchestras and several smaller ensembles for popular music.

In September 1942, a transport arrived from Vienna, and with it an older cellist, Lucian Horwitz (born 1879). He joined in the musical life of the ghetto, although not as an active player. He liked to share his vast musical knowledge and experience with younger musicians as their mentor or—as some of them would refer to him— kibitzer. During the two years he spent in Terezín, Horwitz formed a small string orchestra, mainly from German musicians, and with them he presented several concerts. This ensemble did not compete with the large orchestra of Karel Ančerl, and being of a chamber music type, it concentrated on old music. Horwitz left Terezín on October 28, 1944, with the last transport to Auschwitz, where he died a couple of days later.

In the history of deceit at the Terezín ghetto, one chapter must not be omitted. Among the Jews in Germany, some people were so prominent and well known around the world that the Nazis had to give them special consideration and treatment, rather than send them to their doom in some extermination camp. This privilege applied by law to former army officers who obtained decorations of honor during the First World War. Therefore, instead of arresting them, the Nazis extended to them an invitation to spend the Second World War in the tranquillity of the Terezín "spa" (*Theresienbad*). The promise of comfortable living in elegant hotels, overlooking parks and a lake, and the permission to bring all their valuable belongings, made the offer irresistible. Although the persecution of the Jews in Germany was continuing at an ever increasing rate, there were enough gullible people to take this offer seriously. And so, they came to Terezín, ready to plunge into a busy social life. Instead of practical things, the ladies brought jewelry and gowns, while the gentlemen came attired in dapper full dress suits and top hats. The illusion of the "spa" disappeared like a Fata Morgana the moment they arrived in the ghetto. By the time they passed the thorough inspection, called *Schleusse* or in the Czech adaptation *šlojska,* they were left with the bare necessities, and instead of luxury accommodations with a beautiful view from the window, they were herded into already overcrowded houses in the drab-looking garrison town. The promised social life was exchanged for a busy work schedule, and it must have been a tragicomic sight to see the distinguished looking gentlemen with top hats as they pulled the all-purpose hearse delivering food and corpses.

The only thing faintly resembling a "spa" were the concerts in the musical pavilion in the neglected park on the Terezín square. The ambitious Carlo Taube there led concerts of semiclassical music, very much in the style of the "spa" orchestras popular in prewar Europe. In October 1943 the Danish Jews reached their destination with a transport to Terezín, among them the former conductor of the Royal Orchestra in Copenhagen, Peter Deutsch (born 1901). In the ghetto, he organized the *Stadtkapelle* (town orchestra), very similar to the ensemble of Carlo Taube, and he also gave performances of comparable music on the plaza. Furthermore, the pavilion was shared with the jazz group "Ghetto Swingers," whose activities are described in Chapter XIV.

For the complete picture of the orchestral activities in Terezín, one has to add ensembles put together for special occasions, such as some of the operatic performances of the children's opera *Brundibár,* Pergolesi's *La Serva Padrona,* or Ullmann's novelty, *The Emperor of Atlantis,* which did not reach the stage of public performance.

The quantity of the orchestral ensembles in Terezín and their concert presentations may indicate an overabundance of musical talent and maybe an unnecessarily high number of instrumental groups. This was not really the case, since most of the ensembles were manned by the same people. Of course, there is no question that the musical talent in Terezín was plentiful. The better the musician, the more he was sought after. The violinist Karel Fröhlich was in such demand that he had to serve as concertmaster in all Terezín orchestras!

So, the reason for the existence of all these ensembles lies primarily in the need of the various conductors for their artistic expression. What role their vanity played in having an orchestra bearing the conductor's name is a matter of speculation. Artistic egos, deflated by the conditions in which people found themselves against their own will, pined for any possible boost. Nevertheless, whatever their motivation, the conductors with their orchestras achieved the ultimate goal, that of giving pleasure and enjoyment to audiences of different musical tastes and preferences.

SEVEN

Gideon Klein
and Pavel Haas

Musical life of such magnitude as that of Terezín could not go unnoticed by the imprisoned composers. At the beginning, it was the lack of musical scores that prompted Gideon Klein to arrange countless songs for Rafael Schächter's various choral groups. Except for one Hebrew song, *Bachuri leantisa*, for a female chorus, none of these arrangements are preserved. However, the existing programs and testimony of survivors indicate a large number of such adaptations. The other piece, a Hebrew lullaby, not an original composition of Klein, bears a German title *Wiegenlied*. Klein used a charming old Hebrew folk song and provided a fitting piano accompaniment.

Gideon Klein started to compose as a fifteen-year-old boy. Apparently, his work from that period was influenced by his literary interest in Charles Baudelaire and the Czech poet Otakar Březina. Unfortunately, all his early attempts were lost. Only the results of his creative endeavors from Terezín remain as mementos of his great talent. Obviously, the choice of musical forms and media reflected existing conditions. Aside from the vocal arrangements, Klein wrote

Gideon Klein. Drawing by Petr Kien.

the previously mentioned madrigals, and his other efforts centered around chamber and piano music. The pivotal compositions, which also happened to be his most extensive, are the *String Trio* and *Sonata for Piano*. Both of them, as well as the remaining works from Terezín, demonstrate Klein's mastery of compositional technique, combined with the healthy influence of his paragons, Schoenberg and Janáček. On the other hand, there is no evidence of any influence of his mentor, Alois Hába, the well known exponent of microtonal composition, with whom Klein studied as recently as 1939 and 1940. It was due, no doubt, to purely practical reasons. The artistic growth and development of Gideon Klein the composer cannot be determined, since any comparison between his early compositions and his Terezín output is out of the question. Janáček's influence is most evident in Klein's *Fugue for a String Quartet*, completed on February 2, 1943, and especially in his *Strong Trio*, written in 1944, with haunting variations on a Moravian folk song. The strong affinity with Schoenberg is evident from the atonal concept of the *Sonata for Piano*, perhaps Klein's best composition altogether.

One of the major works composed by Gideon Klein in Terezín but not preserved, was the song cycle *Die Pest* (The Plague). The four songs for alto and piano were written to the poetry of a young fellow prisoner, Petr Kien, who was as talented in painting as in poetry. The songs were performed by Hilde Aronson-Lindt as the opening number of the second concert of the *Studio for New Music*. It is difficult to establish whether this was the premiere performance, since not even the date is known, and also the number of repeats is unknown.

Gideon Klein's readiness to fill artistic needs in the ghetto led him into collaboration in an extraordinary undertaking. The leader of the *Jugendfürsorge* (youth welfare) in Terezín, Egon (better known as Gonda) Redlich, experienced there a change of his own convictions. To his Terezín diary he confided: "Four months in Terezín. Sensation: I am becoming a Jew to all intents and purposes here. The Czech songs and culture are becoming indifferent to me, I am reaching the conviction for which I was heading—to become a real Jew." As a result of this change of heart, Redlich tried his hand at his dramatic first, a kind of monodrama called *The Great Shadow* (*Velký Stín*). It depicted memories of an old Jewish widow who

Autograph of a string trio by Gideon Klein.

found herself suddenly in a concentration camp, unable to answer the burning question: WHY? Vlasta Schönová[23] portrayed the old woman, sitting on the stage and reminiscing of her whole life, while Helena Herrmannová danced the old woman's fantasies to piano music especially composed and played by Gideon Klein. The seriousness with which he approached his work, and the respect he evoked are described in the following words of Mrs. Herrmannová:

> Gideon Klein did in fact compose the music for the play. I remember vividly our rehearsals together, prior to rehearsals with Gonda and Vava, during which we discussed and pooled our ideas on the music and choreography for the play. He had a formidable reputation already at that time, and I had been told that he didn't suffer fools gladly, so I was naturally slightly apprehensive when I met him the first time. As it happened, we worked together very well indeed; he was most sensitive to my ideas and gave me every confidence. As far as I can remember, he wrote down the music and played it at performances from the score, but . . . I don't know what became of it. . . . From the beginning of our preliminary discussions about the play, I felt very happy to be involved in an artistic venture that had its roots in the problems of Terezín, was created there, and by its very theme presented a challenge to performers and audiences alike. I cannot say after all these years whether the play had great literary merit, but I know for sure that it was written with sincerity and conviction, and I believe that it was dramatically sound.[24]

No matter how much effort and work the four artists put into the production of *The Great Shadow*, the play was not accepted with any particular success. The fault presumably resided in the form of the work itself, combined with the author's inexperience in dramatic writing. Both the text and Klein's music were lost, and the history of the play was preserved thanks to memoirs of the two surviving performers, Vlasta Schönová and Helena Herrmannová. Egon

---

[23]The suffix (*ová*) indicates in Czech a female name, thus Schön- (ová). The aforementioned actress changed her name to Vava Šanová, and finally to Nava Shan.
[24]From a letter to the author, August 30, 1977.

Redlich lost his life in the gas chamber of Auschwitz in the fall of 1944, and Gideon Klein died in Fürstengrube at the end of January 1945. His death was an irreparable loss to Czech music. The pianist Truda Reisová-Solarová remembered him in what would be his most eloquent eulogy:

> I met him (Gideon Klein) in Prague, in 1940, when I, a seventeen-year-old girl, started to study under the excellent Czech piano teacher, Professor Vilém Kurz. Gideon, tall, slim, with black hair, vivid but controlled, was of extremely impressive and well-groomed appearance. He was considered to be one of the most talented pupils of Professor Kurz, and despite his youth had a distinct personal, developed touch. His outstanding intelligence, his great interest for many different branches of art, for literature, and especially for music, so impressed all who knew him that it seemed as if some strange magic emanated from his personality. All of us, without reserve, admitted the superiority of Gideon Klein, maybe just because he did not try to be better than we were: he was.[25]

As a moving spirit behind the musical activities in Terezín, Klein has to his credit the emergence of another prominent composer, Pavel Haas. A man in his forties, Haas came to Terezín with undermined health. The miserable conditions there further affected his severe depressions, resulting in total indifference to the very busy musical life of Terezín. According to his sister, Eliška (Lisa), Gideon Klein could not reconcile himself to seeing an artist of Haas' caliber not participating in the musical activities. So, one day, to wake him from his lethargy, Klein put in front of him several sheets of manuscript paper, on which he himself drew the musical staff, and urged Haas to stop wasting time. And indeed, Haas composed several pieces during his stay in Terezín, although only three of them have been preserved.

By the time Pavel Haas came to Terezín among the first deportees in 1941, he was already an accomplished and recognized composer. He was born in the Moravian capital, Brno, on June 6, 1899, as the

[25]Reprinted with permission from the book *Terezín*.

first-born son of a well-to-do businessman. Although his father, Zikmund, was a Czech Jew and his mother (née Epstein) came from Russia, young Pavel had to go to German schools, and, in a city with a large German population, he became associated with German-speaking friends. With a one-year interruption, he finished his lower secondary education at the Czech institution, but in his early teens his strong interest in music led him to enroll in the Music School of the Philharmonic Society (*Beseda*) in Brno. From this period originate Haas' first attempts in composition.

Besides a larger number of completed songs, all using German text, Haas showed a trait which did not leave him for the rest of his life: the frequent failure to finish compositions. He started several larger works, including a piano quartet, symphony, and even an opera, but his lack of professional training and experience left the audacious plans in their embryonic stage. Haas' compositions from the years 1912–16 show his strong affinity with German romanticism. The influence of his Czech music mentors, Jan Kunc and Vilém Petrželka, became evident for the first time in two songs written in 1917. That year he also had to exchange his pen for a rifle, being drafted into the Austrian army. Luckily for him, Haas never saw combat and stayed in Brno until the end of the war. After the cessation of hostilities, Haas resumed his musical studies at the newly established State Conservatory in Brno, and in 1920 he joined the class of Leoš Janáček at the Master School there.

The strength of Janáček's creative power caused a complete turnaround in Haas' musical thinking. Following the footsteps of his master, Haas found the nucleus of his musical perception in a folk song, another trait which remained with him during his entire lifetime, except for a short interlude when he became exposed for the first time to the music of the French "*Les Six*".[26] From this time also begins Haas' involvement in incidental music for dramatic productions of the Provincial Theater in Brno. From here, the next logical step led Haas to writing music for films, no doubt due to the

[26]"*Les Six*" was a group of six French composers of the 1920s, which included Arthur Honnegger, Darius Milhaud, Francis Poulenc, Louis Durey, Georges Auric, and Germaine Tailleferre.

Pavel Haas. Drawing by Petr Kien.

fact that his younger brother, Hugo, pursued a successful career as a movie actor, first in Czechoslovakia and later in Hollywood. One can also logically deduce that the artistic conversion of Pavel Haas was the result of patriotic enthusiasm, which went hand in hand with the formation of the new independent Czechoslovak Republic in October 1918, after three hundred years of Hapsburg oppression.

The musical output of Pavel Haas in the twenty years between the two world wars is not very large, and it is characterized by a conspicuous number of unfinished works. This was caused possibly by frequent commissions for theater and film music, possibly because Haas had to supplement his income by working in his father's shoestore. Nevertheless, by the time of the Nazi occupation of Czechoslovakia, Haas held a distinguished position on the Czechoslovak musical horizon as one of the foremost disciples of Leos Janáček.

As the Nazi menace drew nearer and nearer, Haas underwent still another artistic transformation, although not as drastic as the first one. While his source of inspiration in the last two decades lay in the Moravian folk song, his compositions from the fearful years 1939–41 are marked by Haas' adherance to the old Czech chorale to St. Wenceslaus, combined with somewhat related elements of Hebraic music, and also the Hussite chorale *Ye Warriors of the Lord (Ktož sú Boží bojovníci)*. This in itself would not be very unusual, because Czech composers turned to these melodies throughout centuries at times of war and oppression, most notably in Smetana's symphonic poems *Tábor* and *Blaník*, and Josef Suk's *Meditation on the Ancient Czech Chorale*. What makes it noteworthy in the case of Pavel Haas is the fact that here was a Jewish composer finding solace in invocations: "Let us not perish, us and our descendents, Saint Wenceslaus!" It is even more thought-provoking in view of the fact that Haas' widow described him as politically oriented to the left. The St. Wencelsaus theme emerges from the entire *Suite for Oboe and Piano*, written in 1939, as well as his unfinished symphony, on which he worked in the ensuing two years.

Pavel Haas went to Terezín alone. He formally divorced his wife and thus saved her and their young daughter from a concentration

Title page of Pavel Haas' composition for a male chorus, *Al S'fod*.

camp. Haas' wife, in turn, took care of the infant nephew left behind by Hugo, who was able to emigrate to Hollywood.

From the time when Pavel Haas renewed his creative activities until his departure and immediate execution in Auschwitz, on October 17, 1944, he produced a respectable number of new compositions. However, even this period discloses his ever present idiosyncrasy: unfinished work. Only three pieces are in existence today. The male chorus *Al S'fod* was completed on November 30, 1942, and was dedicated to the Deputy Chairman of the Terezín Council of Elders, Otto Zucker. The choice of text shows the determination of the composer not to succumb to the tyranny of the spirit. *Al S'fod* is based on a poem by an Israeli author Jakov Simoni, who had written it during the Arab-Israeli skirmishes in 1936–39. Haas, who did not know Hebrew, apparently used for his model the musical rendition of J. Millet, in order to get a better idea of the Hebrew accent. The first two lines sum up the whole context in the words: "Do not lament, do not cry, when things are bad, do not lose heart, but work, work!"

A little curiosity appears on the title page of the manuscript. Musical notes, adapted to look like Hebrew letters and placed carefully on the staff, exclaim longingly: *Mizkeret lejon hasana harison vemu acharon begalut Terezín* (In remembrance of the first and at the same time last anniversary of the Terezín exile). It is questionable whether Haas alone made the inscription or if somebody helped him with it. The work contains unmistakably Hebraic elements, but, upon closer examination, one can recognize related motives from the chorale to St. Wenceslaus.

The same motives are much more evident in the excellent cycle *Four Songs to the Text of Chinese Poetry*, written between February and April 1944. The young basso Karel Berman was readying his recital of lieder by Beethoven, Dvořák, and Hugo Wolf. For a greater variety, he requested some songs from Haas, who at first was very reluctant about the project, but then he quickly furnished the singer with what is perhaps his best Terezín composition. Haas could easily identify with the words of Chinese poets in the Czech translation by Bohumil Mathesius, expressing loneliness, homesickness, and hope for a happy return home. The composer's

KONCERTNÍ SÍŇ V RADNICI
22. ČERVNA 1944.

PÍSŇOVÝ KONCERT

K. BERMANN —— bas
R. SCHÄCHTER — klavír

PROGRAM

H. WOLF:
3 PÍSNĚ NA TEXTY MICHELANGELOVY

L. van BEETHOVEN:
VZDÁLENÉ MILÉ

P. HAAS:
4 PÍSNĚ NA SLOVA ČÍNSKÉ POESIE (MATHESIUS)
PRVNÍ PROVEDENÍ

A. DVOŘÁK:
CIGÁNSKÉ MELODIE

Program of a recital of Karel Berman on June 22, 1944.

attendance during the rehearsals certainly contributed to a very successful premiere, in May of the same year, when Berman presented his recital in the hall of the former City Hall, accompanied masterfully by Rafael Schächter on the piano. In one of his most enthusiastic reactions to a musical performance, Viktor Ullmann wrote:

> The eloquent, courageous, all-around talented artist, singer, composer, conductor, Karel Berman, was until today a journeyman—now he has delivered his masterpiece. If one must thank him, right at the beginning, for an exemplary, distinguished, and well chosen program, then it is the next duty to express an enthusiastic thanks also to Pavel Haas for his beautiful gift: his *Four Songs to Chinese Poetry*, premiered on this evening.
>
> . . . Once one has heard them, one would not want to miss Haas' topical songs so full of life, and live with them in intimate relationship. For only this way can new art succeed in the course of time: it becomes house music and an indispensable friend, like a good book, like everything that one acquires with practice. An especially lucky hit is the graceful, bright, and rhythmically pulsating second song of the cycle, which turns up later once more in the fourth song as the Coda of the whole work, and brings it to conclusion. However, even these earnest songs, yearning for home—in which the first and third are linked with each other by an *idée fixe* of four tones that returns as *ostinato* or *cantus firmus* in manifold metamorphoses—are the result of an impressive, genuine, and still progressive inspiration. Stylistically, the Haas songs are very personal. . . . The harmony is not expressionistic, although dissonant chords prevail, but they are subordinated to a latent tonal center. Berman recreated the cycle with utmost musicianship and with a fine sense for the characteristic musical language, as well as being vocally expressive; Rafael Schächter was an affectionate and understanding interpreter at the piano.

With this kind of reception, it is no wonder that Berman had to repeat his program several times before his departure for Auschwitz the following October.

The third and last preserved composition written by Pavel Haas in Terezín is the *Study for Strings*. It came into existence as the composer's contribution to the otherwise scanty repertoire of Karel Ančerl's string orchestra. The complicated score made heavy demands on the players with its difficult rhythmical patterns, syncopation, frequent changes of time signatures and tempo, and dividing of the regular orchestral sections. The *Study* proves the artistic integrity of the composer, who did not lower his ideals no matter how adverse the conditions. Although Haas composed this work in 1943, Ančerl did not prepare it for the premiere until the summer of 1944, first during the filming of the propaganda movie made in Terezín by the Nazis, and then in the actual concert premiere, just a few days before the last big transports took practically the entire orchestra to Auschwitz.

The original score of the *Study for Strings* was lost. However, after the war, Ančerl found the orchestral parts in Terezín, all except for the bass part. He helped Professor Lubomír Peduzzi, a friend of Haas' family, to reconstruct the new score, but he did not conduct the composition again.

At least two additional compositions of Pavel Haas were offered to the Terezín public: *Fantasy on a Jewish Folk Song* for string quartet and *Partita in the Old Style* for piano. The former was played by the Ledeč Quartet, the latter came to life under the fingers of Haas' longtime friend, Bernard Kaff. Among works not performed remained *Variations for Piano and String Orchestra*, probably the last completed work, and a cycle of three songs for mezzo soprano, tenor, and several instruments, called *The Advent*. For the victims of the Nazi persecution, Haas intended a grandiose *Requiem for Soloists, Chorus, and Orchestra*, which apparently had not progressed beyond the preliminary sketches at the time of Haas' death.

EIGHT

Education through Music

In children the nation is eternal. Destroy them, and in a few decades the nation—or we may substitute the race—will be reduced to a few paragraphs in a history book, and culture will be attested through a few museum collections. This is what the Nazis planned for the Jews, and this is why they kept documents and mementos of what they expected to become an extinct race. This is also the reason the Jewish children became unwilling pawns in the inconspicuous, undeclared warfare between the leaders of the Czech Jewish community and their Nazi oppressors.

As the first logical step in this direction, the Germans deprived the Jewish children of normal education. However, a kind of loophole was left in some Jewish institutions, such as orphanages. There the youngsters were cared for by young educators, members of the Zionist socialist organization, which came to life in Czech lands even before the outbreak of the war. Its combined headquarters and collective living quarters were in Prague, on the street Na Zderaze No. 14. Besides to a certain degree normal school instruction, the

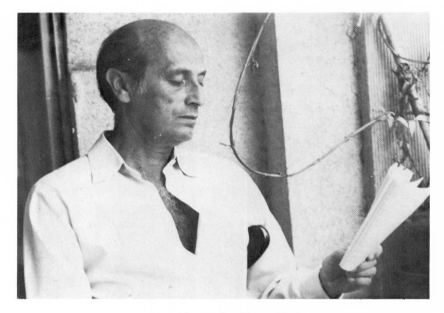

Ambassador Zeev Shek.

wards participated in choral groups (*Pěvecké sdružení*) and also had
the opportunity to hear recitation of poetry and dramas as well as
discussions on various topics. The latter bordered on illegality or
were outright violations of the law when the subject happened to
deal with Zionistic endeavors. Not surprisingly, these discussions in
particular were the most lively and popular.

As the children were being moved to Terezín, the need for
educators there became more pressing and, at the same time, less
important in the cities. The chairman of the Jewish Council of Elders
in Terezín, Jakob Edelstein, convinced some of these teachers that
they should volunteer for duty in the ghetto. One of the last to do so
was Zeev Shek, one of the protagonists of the Hechalutz movement.
He came to Terezín sometime in October 1943. By that time, the
majority of the children lived there already. Shek was officially

assigned to some job in the ghetto, but his real mission was to care once more for the children. He was also elected in a secret meeting to the executive council of the illegal Hechalutz movement in Terezín.

This time, the situation was very different from the previous one in Prague. The Nazis forbade any kind of teaching in the ghetto but insisted on keeping the children busy. Shek was in charge of youngsters between fourteen and eighteen years of age, who had to work during the day. Only children under fourteen had been exempted from working except for occasional "help duty" (*Hilfsdienst*).

The Council of Elders together with the leaders of the Hechalutz realized the necessity of giving the children education, even at the risk of disobeying the Nazi command. After many meetings and arguments, the educators developed a system of teaching without actually breaking the law. This is how Zeev Shek describes it:

So, I came to the *útulek* (children's home). I had about twenty children in my room who had not enough to eat, and now I had to keep them busy. The Germans called it *Beschäftigung*. I could play with them, I could sing with them, but I was not allowed to teach them. So, we had to invent ways. And here our education of scouting, of youth movement, has helped a lot. Maybe you will remember that in one of Kipling's books which is called *Kim*, they play "Kim games," games of observation. Or they play *Slavní muži* (Famous men). So, we had a system of teaching history by playing "Famous Men." Or you know the game "Countries and towns." You say a town and the other must say the country. Or you say, it starts with P and ends with A; it's PRAHA (Prague). This was geography. And we even had a system for smaller children. Singing was also a way of teaching. We took Hebrew songs, which were based on poems, and so we had a little of literature. It was not easy and it was not, of course, unanimous what to teach. Some friends believed that we should give these children a Czech education, not a Jewish education. We had children from Denmark, from Germany. But we were sure that we had to give them a Jewish education, universal but Jewish, by all means not chauvinistic. They were in the ghetto and we wanted to bring these children out of the ghetto spiritually, mentally sane, so that they would become quite normal people. I would call it "positivistic approach to life," this normalization under abnormal circumstances, giving all these people a kind of belief that under any circumstances, you are a human being, and it is up to you to react as a human being. They can break your body; they can't break your spirit without your cooperation. This is what we used to tell them. After all, the logical way to fight death is to stay alive, isn't it?[27]

Although Zeev Shek was primarily a teacher of Hebrew, he considered music as an inseparable constituent of general education. Being endowed with a naturally pleasant lyric tenor, he took voice lessons with Madame Zeckendorf in Prague. His repertoire centered around the music of Old Masters, Beethoven, Pergolesi and the like. Later, after the war, as a member of the Israeli diplomatic service, he made it his practice to learn folk songs of the country of each of his assignments.[28]

The important role singing played in the education of children becomes obvious from the choice of music. Special emphasis was given to Jewish patriotic songs. It served a dual purpose: resistance to tyranny and boosting the pride of being Jewish. In this vein Shek explained to the little boys that the yellow star on their breast is the star from heaven, the star of Judas Maccabeus, and to the older charges he pointed out the achievement of the Jewish Nobel Prize winners. To foster interest in the Zionist movement, the youngsters learned to sing Hechalutz songs, while folk songs were used simply because youth movements tend naturally to favor folklore.

It should be noted that under Shek's leadership, children sang in Hebrew, Czech, and German. Any criticism of the latter language he brushes aside this way:

I was always against boycotting of the German language, because I was of the opinion that the language is the vehicle. It is not the

[27]Transcribed from a taped interview with the author, in Jerusalem, on January 5, 1977.
[28]Mr. Zeev Shek died in Rome on October 2, 1978 (Rosh Hashana) while serving there as Ambassador of Israel.

language that is bad, it's what you say that's bad. The first anti-Semitic writings of modern times were in English. It was (Houston Stewart) Chamberlain, the English racist and philosopher. The Roman and Greek anti-Semites did not write in German, while, on the other hand, Theodor Herzl wrote *Der Judestaat* in German. So, we also sang German songs.[29]

In this manner, the youngsters were exposed, perhaps unintentionally, to three languages on top of the musical content. The use of canon songs led to better understanding of musical theory. A canon is a basic polyphonic device consisting of two or more independent voices, in which one part is imitated in its entirety by others at a short distance of one measure or so. The simplest kind of canon are songs sung in rounds. In this field, Shek had substantial help from the professional pianist, Tella Polák, and in collaboration with her they even presented an evening of canon songs in Terezín.

Last, but by no means least, singing of chassidic and liturgical songs was used in Terezín to deepen the religious education. Zeev Shek learned from his father a variety of such songs and even purchased a book which he eventually brought to Terezín. Thus, during the Channukah festival, he would choose a boy and a girl to light the candles while he sang the *bracha* (blessings) strumming gently a borrowed guitar. He had learned the beautiful melody as a lad of sixteen from his father in his native Olomouc (Moravia). It had been sung by the local cantor, Perlman, who apparently adapted it from some other Hassan.[30]

New songs and ditties expressing the resistance to the tyranny had sprung up frequently in the ghetto, and sometimes these were composed for a particular occasion. Children from the "youth home" in the "Brandenburg" barracks celebrated appropriately the feast of Purim in 1943 with the following song by an unknown author:

[29]Transcription from a taped interview with the author. See note 22.
[30]Hebrew word for cantor.

The play is over,
The workday begins,
A grey wall obscures the sun from us.

Troubles are we piling up,
And in captivity we are wailing;
Rage and hatred close the world to us.

But once the day will arrive
When we'll walk out of the ghetto,
And life will smile at us.

In defiance of the Hamans
We will break the bars.
Forward our hope leads us.

Children sang in various ensembles, such as the children's chorus, directed by Rudolf Freudenfeld, or the girls' chorus of Karel Berman. Those who showed special promise in the field of music would be sent to Rafael Schächter or Karel Berman for further musical training and the chance to participate in the adult musical activities.

The most elaborate musical undertaking for children was the presentation of two children's operas, *Bastien and Bastienne* by Mozart, and *Brundibár* by Hans Krása. *Bastien and Bastienne* was performed thirty times under the baton of Hans (sometimes spelled Heinz) Jochowitz. Viktor Ullmann, in his undated review of the premiere, praised Karel Berman for the first fully staged operatic performance in Terezín. The sets for this production had been designed by the architect František Zelenka, formerly of the National Theater in Prague. Berman also prepared the vocalists. Bastien was portrayed by H. Tomková, Bastienne by R. Fuchsová, and the role of Colas was entrusted to a young amateur, Karel Polák, who died later in the concentration camp in Kauffering. The entire production was accompanied by a string quartet comprised of the violinists Kling and Block, the violist Parkus, and the cellist Dauber.

The history of *Brundibár* is extensive and deserves a detailed explanation in the following chapter.

Musical education of children did not consist only of singing. Young instrumentalists were encouraged to take lessons from their older peers. Pavel Kling recalls his violin studies with Karel Fröhlich, augmented by coaching from the pianist Bernard Kaff and theory lessons with the composer Pavel Haas. Kling developed a rather robust violin sound, because instead of a real violin, he was handed the only available instrument, a smaller viola with violin strings attached.

But even more important than all the music lessons was the participation in the orchestra and chamber ensembles. As Kling expressed it, he "absorbed everything like a sponge." The violinist Tomáš Mandl, remembers how Kaff brought him a book and music when he was sick with scarlet fever, and how he, as a boy of fifteen, "blackmailed" deputy chairman Otto Zucker to lend him his violin. The talented youngsters received all possible help in the form of employment in the office, so that they would not ruin their hands and, above all, they could have time to develop their talent through diligent practicing.

Having been involved in education most of his life, Bernard Kaff ran in Terezín a miniature private conservatory. Obviously, his students did not have money for the lessons, so they had to "pay" with their services. Once a week, they had to come to Kaff's little room and clean it. For greater efficiency, they even formed a special organization, in jest called PIPO, an abbreviation for *Pianistenpolizei* (pianists police), whose task was the supervision of the fullest utilization of available pianos for practicing purposes.

Music history and aesthetics were taught mainly through discussions and lectures by people such as Dr. H. G. Adler or Dr. James Simon, to which the young adepts listened attentively with eager ears. Budding composers had the chance to study theory and composition with several outstanding composers who were very willing to share their knowledge. Jiří Kummermann of Prague met his death in Auschwitz at the age of fifteen. The last part of his life he spent in Terezín, where he studied piano with Kaff, and in little more than a year he wrote ninety-nine pages of exercises in harmony and counterpoint. The corrections of his unknown teacher indicate the student's command of harmony, while the counterpoint apparently was not exactly his forte.

For a number of future artists, Terezín became not only a great school, a conservatory. It was a place where they had the opportunity to try their fledgling wings on their upsurge to artistic heights. For others it meant only great expectations and ruthlessly unfulfilled dreams.

Poster for Hans Krása's children's opera, *Brundibár*.

NINE

Brundibár

The origins of the children's opera *Brundibár* date back to the years before the outbreak of the war. When the Nazi sympathizers in Czechoslovakia started to raise their voices calling for the annexation to the Third Reich, the German-speaking supporters of the republic showed their solidarity by seeking new Czech friends and joining or forming with them new organizations and clubs for the purpose of extending mutual interests. In this manner, Hans Krása met the playwright of the Czech leftist avant-garde, Adolf Hoffmeister, and sometime in 1938 they wrote the children's opera for a competition of the Ministry of Education and Culture. It was their second joint venture since 1935, when Krása composed incidental music to Hoffmeister's play *Mládí re hye (Youth in the Game)*.

The original score of *Brundibár* had been lost, and only the piano reduction was available at the time of the Nazi occupation. Much later, in 1972, a calligraphic copy of the original score was found and donated to the Memorial Terezín. From that it became obvious that Krása had entered the competition anonymously, perhaps on the basis of his previous success in 1933, when he became a recipient of the Czechoslovak State Prize for Composition for his German opera *Verlobung im Traum* (Betrothal in Dream). However, it is doubtful

Hans Krása. Drawing by Petr Kien.

Sketch of the set for *Brundibár* by František Zelenka.

Brundibár. Photo of the actual performance of Krása's children's opera in Terezín for the International Red Cross Committee.

that he could repeat this feat. For one thing, Hoffmeister's libretto is rather naive, and poetically leaves much to be desired. Even though he apparently tried to imitate the talk of children, this does not excuse gross violations of verbal accent and ictus and frequent crude rhymes, achieved through cheap use of Czech diminutives. At the same time, Krása was a German-speaking and educated Czechoslovak citizen, who, although he had knowledge of the Czech language, did not have always the feeling for the subtleties of the Czech accent. Thus his score bears signs of deficiency. However, the music itself is so buoyant, melodic, and charming that it easily makes up for the inadequacies. It should be noted that the competition never took place, undoubtedly due to the political developments in the country.

One of the meeting places of the Prague Jews after their expulsion from public life was the Jewish orphanage called Hagibor. Its director, Rudolf Freudenfeld, Sr., himself an avid music lover and amateur singer, fostered the musical activities of his wards, especially when formal education was prohibited. Freudenfeld had always had an ambition to sing liturgical music. Since printed material was not available, his son, Rudolf, Jr., arranged some chants for solo basso with the accompaniment of children's chorus and, on one occasion, even Jerome Kern's *Ol'Man River*. The youngsters participated also in bigger productions, including children's operas, *Wir bauen eine Stadt*, (We are building a city) by Paul Hindemith, and *The Fat Great-grandfather, Robbers and Detectives* by the Czech composer Jaroslav Křička.

In July 1941, the director Freudenfeld celebrated his fiftieth birthday. Of course, an occasion like this would not be complete without a musical program. On that day, the wellwishers included the conductor Rafael Schächter, composer Hans Krása, pianist Gideon Klein, poet Emil A. Saudek, and the stage director from the National Theater, architect František Zelenka. Schächter informed his colleagues that Krása's opera *Brundibár* had not been performed as yet, and immediately steps were taken to rectify this omission. With his typical energy, Schächter immediately started serious weekly rehearsals, assisted by the director's son.

Schächter did not stay in Prague long enough to conduct the premiere of *Brundibá*r. On November 27, 1941, he went to Terezín. The young Freudenfeld took over completely, and the first performance was staged in the orphanage dining room. Zelenka designed not only the set but the whole stage. This was quite dangerous in case of a Nazi surprise visit, because such an activity was forbidden. And, as a matter of fact, the unwelcome visitors actually came one day while the stage was erected. Luckily, the director diverted their attention enough to avoid opening of the fateful door.

Zelenka was also entrusted with the directing of the opera. His ingeniously conceived set consisted of several boards forming a fence. Three posters with pictures of a dog, a cat, and a swallow were hanging on it, all with holes instead of the head. At appropriate times, the performers would stick their heads through these holes and sing the roles of the animals. As a joke, Zelenka added another poster with the inscription, "Volte 62541," (Vote for 62541), which was the telephone number of the Jewish Community in Prague. The entire production was accompanied by three instrumentalists in lieu of the whole orchestra: pianist Löffelholz, violinist Berkovič, and drummer Kaufman. Since they did not have either the full score or individual parts, all of them, including the conductor, had to look into the same piano reduction.

The story of the opera deals with two little children, Little Joe and Annette (Pepíček and Aninka), who have a sick mother. The doctor prescribed milk for her, but they had no money to buy it. Seeing the organ-grinder, Brundibár, as he plays on the street corner, they start singing, to the annoyance of the passers-by and Brundibár, who chases them away. Three animals, a dog, a cat, and a sparrow, come to their help. Together with the children from the neighborhood, they sing a charming lullaby, and people give them money. However, in an unguarded moment, Brundibár steals it from them. All children and animals chase him and recover the money. The opera ends with a song of victory over the evil organ-grinder.

The premiere of the opera, which took place during the winter 1942–43, met with great success, although only some 150 people could attend. By that time not only Schächter but also Krása and Zelenka had been sent to Terezín. After a repeat performance the children began to be enrolled in the Terezín transports, and in July 1943 the last of them, together with their "Boss," Freudenfeld, and his son, were reunited once more. By this time, Schächter's musical activities were in full swing, and he honored Freudenfeld with a special performance of *The Bartered Bride*. In return, Freudenfeld presented the vocal score of *Brundibár* to Schächter.

Erna Grünfeld, who had witnessed the first performance of *Brundibá*r in the Prague orphanage, sent word to her fiancé, Rafael Schächter, about the praiseworthy presentation. As a result, he in turn entrusted the younger Freudenfeld once more with the production of the opera.

The rehearsals were being held in the attic of Block L 417, originally a school, and at that time a home for boys, with the accompaniment of a harmonium. For the title roles of Little Joe and Annette, Shächter recommended two of his "seasoned veterans," Pinťa Mühlstein, the "bear" from *The Bartered Bride,* and twelve-year-old Greta Hofmeister, member of his opera chorus. The first dog was played by Zdeněk Ornest, the pussycat by Eva Stein, and the sparrow by the six-year-old son of the pianist Alice Herz-Sommer, Rafael. The ungrateful role of the organ-grinder fell to Honza Treichlinger, an orphan from Plzeň (Pilsen), who actually asked for it when he met the conductor in the washroom. On the basis of his portrayal, Honza became a Terezín "celebrity." Rudolf Freudenfeld, Jr., describes his unusual talent in his article about *Brundibár:*

> Brundibár is a negative hero. He is a wicked old man, an organ-grinder who does not want to let the children sing for money in the district which he considers his beat. In the end he steals their purse with the collected money. It is a character full of mental conflict for children, who always have sympathy for beggars and poor people; but this one was wicked, ugly. Honza, quite instinctively, made the character of Brundbár so human that although he played a wicked character, he became the darling of the audience. He learned to twitch the whiskers which we stuck under his nose. He twitched them so well, and at just the right time, that tension relaxed in the auditorium, and often we could hear the children releasing their bated breath.
>
> From the moment in which he "made" the character, he played all performances without understudy. Anybody else would have failed.
>
> What might he have become? Actor or engineer? How he could have humanized his own life as he had his role! That he was rather short was fateful to him.[31] He was fourteen years old. He went to Auschwitz with the old and the small children and directly into the gas chamber.[32]

---

[31]Reference to the selection of children in Auschwitz: those who could not reach a string stretched above their heads had to go to the gas chambers.
[32]Reprinted with permission from the book *Terezín.*

The premiere of *Brundibár* in Terezín took place on September 23, 1943,[33] in the "Magdeburg" barracks. František Zelenka was once again responsible for the staging and directing, almost identical with the performance in Prague, and he was assisted by the choreographer Kamila Rosenbaum.

Opinion has been voiced in a number of publications about the ever-changing cast, as a result of the transports leaving for Auschwitz. It is true that some of the children, mainly in the chorus, had to be occasionally replaced. However, the three main characters, Brundibár, Little Joe, and Annette, played in all performances. At the end of September and in October 1944, almost all the children were sent to the much feared East, to pay the ultimate sacrifice to the Nazi Moloch. Honza Treichlinger and Pintă Mühlstein did not return; some of the others were more lucky.

Similarly, conflicting stories circulate about the accompaniment. The conductor, Rudolf Freudenfeld, writes in his memoirs that all performances in Terezín were presented with orchestra. This contradicts sharply the reminiscences of Greta Hofmeister, the Terezín Annette, who believes that a harmonium was always used. Dr. Kurt Singer, a noted German musicologist from Berlin, attended one of the performances, and in his review he mentioned the accompaniment of a small orchestra. Considering the time of his death in Terezín, in January 1944, (he was born October 11, 1885 in Breent), this would support the conductor's assertion.

Hans Krása wrote in Terezín a new orchestral score from the only available piano reduction. Tailor-made for the instrumentalists at hand, it called for a flute, a clarinet, a trumpet, a guitar, an accordion, a piano, percussions, four violins, cello, and bass. The orchestra was a truly virtuoso group with members such as the violinist Karel Fröhlich, pianist Gideon Klein, cellist Fredy Mark, clarinetist Fritz Weiss, the Kohn brothers, etc.

---

[33]The American premiere of *Brundibár* (in Czech) took place in West Hartford, Connecticut, on April 8, 1975; the world premiere of the English version, in the translation of Milada Javora and Joža Karas, was held in Ottawa, Canada, on November 14, 1977, thanks to the tireless efforts of the late Dr. Hugo Fischer and his wife, Dr. Gretl Fischer. Both presentations were conducted by Joza Karas.

Brundibár achieved an unbelievable number of performances—fifty-five altogether. The original production had been moved from the small auditorium in the "Magdeburg" barracks to the large gym hall, called Sokolovna, which was equipped with a modern stage, a pit for the orchestra, and make-up rooms. The camp commander did not like the stage design, because it seemed to him too dark and somber. So, Zelenka with his helpers obtained all necessary material, and in one day they built a brand new set with bright, cheerful colors. In this arrangement the opera was presented until September 1944.

As a children's opera, *Brundibár* met all the requirements of an ideal work in its category. Dr. Kurt Singer recognized its merits, and in a review which he let circulate in the ghetto, he evaluated it in these words:

> *Brundibár* shows how a short opera of today should look and sound, how it can unite the highest in artistic taste with originality of concept, and modern character with viable tunes. We have here a theme which has appeal for children and grown-ups alike, a moral plot motif recalling the old fairy tales, popular singing kept simple in choral sections but occasionally becoming quite complex in duets and trios, and a sensitive balance of dynamics maintained between a dozen instruments and three dozen singers. We have also a Czech national coloration, music-making without recourse to modern experimentation (at which Krása is a master), a clever balance of scenic effects between the orchestra pit and the stage, an orchestra used with taste and economy and a singing line which is never obscured or smothered by the instruments. . . . In this little opera, born of a serious mind and yet so pleasant to the ear, idea and form, thought and preparation, concept and execution are joined in a fruitful marriage of mutual collaboration: Whether it be cast in a large or small form, whether it be song or symphony, chorus or opera, there can be no higher praise for a work of art.[34]

---

[34]Reprinted with permission from the book *The Jews of Czechoslovakia*.

Of all the musical activities in Terezín, *Brundibár* easily became the top attraction. Although there was no charge, admission was by tickets only, and they were not easy to obtain, since the demand was tremendous. There are stories about barter of the tickets or cases of flattery. An older man once came up to Freudenfeld and exclaimed: *"Das ist nicht möglich! Von hinten sind Sie der ganze Toscanini."* (That's not possible! From the rear you are Toscanini all over.) Of course, he hoped to see still another performance.

It became almost a status symbol in the concentration camp to attend this particular opera. The reason is quite obvious. Krása's music is very charming, melodious and easy to understand, even though it bears modern elements. The children represented the hope for the future, while the story itself acquired a political connotation. The mean Brundibár personified Evil. When the children started to sing the final chorus: "Brundibár defeated, we got him already . . . ," there was no doubt in the minds of all present that they were singing about Hitler himself. To make the point even more obvious, the poet Emil A. Saudek altered the very last few lines of the opera, to express the universal feeling of resistance and the ultimate belief in justice. While the original said, "He who loves so much his mother and father and his native land is our friend and he can play with us," Saudek's version read: "He who loves justice and will abide by it, and who is not afraid, is our friend and can play with us."

What can one add to that?

TEN

Hans Krása

The enormous success of *Brundi-bár* prompted its creator, Hans Krása, to a more intensive participation in the musical life of the Terezín Ghetto. As a member of the *Freizeitgestaltung,* he was the head of the entire music section; being an accomplished pianist, he joined the string ensemble in the performance of *La Serva Padrona*; and, above all, as a composer, he enlarged the Terezín repertoire by three new compositions and two new versions of older works. This in itself does not look like a great feat, but for a man used to an easygoing Bohemian style of living, it was quite an accomplishment. After all, in his entire adult life as composer, he had produced only about a dozen compositions.

Hans Krása was born in Prague on November 30, 1899, as the third child of a prosperous Czech attorney and a German-speaking mother. This resulted in his German upbringing and education, combined with loyalty to the Czech cause and the new Republic, and his passionate love for the "Hundred-spired Mother Prague," love for which he ultimately paid with his life.

From an early age, the boy showed an extraordinary musical talent. He started taking piano lessons at the school of Theresie Wallerstein at the age of six. In a short time he caught up with his favorite sister, Marie, three years his senior. For years to come, the

Hans Krása.

two enjoyed playing arrangements of symphonies and overtures for four hands. While Marie, fondly called Mitzi, liked Haydn and Mozart, the more sophisticated Hans prefered works of Schubert, Beethoven, and especially Gustav Mahler. In order to expand Hans' musical horizons further, his understanding father bought him a genuine Amati violin for his tenth birthday and arranged violin lessons with the concertmaster of the German opera house in Prague, Frankenbusch.

Into this period fall also the first attempts of the budding composer. Krása's early pieces were written completely in the style of Haydn and Mozart. When he "composed," Hans did not tolerate anybody in the room. Luckily, it did not cause any particular problem, because the Krása family enjoyed living in a very large apartment with two grand pianos in separate rooms. The walls of the old building were so thick that they made the rooms virtually soundproof. Interestingly enough, Hans did not like to share his compositions with others, not even members of his own family, and only seldom consented, reluctantly, to play for them.

Success came easily to Hans Krása, the composer, thanks primarily to his father's funds and connections. When Hans wrote his first orchestral piece, at the age of eleven, the spa orchestra in Salzburg put it on the program, being hired, no doubt, by the elder Krása. Then, three years later, in 1913, Hans composed a string quartet, and once again his father paid for a professional performance by members of a spa orchestra in the Swiss town of St. Moritz, where the whole Krása family was spending the summer vacation. The whereabouts of all of Krása's compositions from his childhood are unknown.

While pursuing his secondary education, Krása became enamored of the French literary giants Maupassant, Verlaine, Stendhal, and Pascal. Influenced by his sister Franci, he also took great interest in the novels of Dostoyevsky and, to a lesser degree, some English authors. On the other hand, the German writers bored him.

After the completion of his liberal arts studies, Krása devoted himself to music. Even before his graduation from the German Music Academy, he accepted a position as vocal coach at the New German Theater in Prague, under the conductor Alexander

Zemlinsky. This beloved master became Krása's most influential mentor, first at the State Conservatory and later at the newly established Academy. At that time, Krása's individualistic style made an impression. It was characterized by brevity, irony, humor verging on comicality, and grotesqueness. These elements were already evident in Krása's graduation work, *Four Orchestral Songs, op. 1*, based on the "Gallow Songs" (*Galgenlieder*) of the German poet Christian Morgenstern. The songs had their premiere in May 1921, under the baton of Zemlinsky himself, and received praise from several of the most important critics, not only in Prague but even abroad.

Shortly after the war, modern French music found its way into the musical life in Prague. Debussy, Ravel, and the avant-gardists known as "*Les Six*" were quite frequently performed, as well as music of Stravinsky, Schoenberg, Webern, Bartók, and from the Czech composers, Janáček. The musical language of each of them was meaningful to the impressionable developing talent of Hans Krása. Debussy offered new orchestral sound, Stravinsky neoclassical limpidity, Webern brevity, and "*Les Six*" humor, grotesquerie, and irony through use of jazz in serious music, elements closest to Krása's character.

Krása loved the French, and the French accepted him. In April 1923, he scored a double success in Paris with a pastorale and march from his symphony, and shortly after with his first string quartet. On that occasion, the French critic Emil Vuillermoz put Krása into the category of the utmost masters, Schoenberg, Bartók, and Webern. The composer's renown was further enhanced by the performance of the symphony at the festival of contemporary music in Zurich in 1926.

The following year, Zemlinsky had been appointed as conductor at the Berlin State Opera. Krása followed him there to continue his studies of orchestral composition at the Berlin Conservatory. Disappointed, however, he returned home after two semesters. The only bright spot of that sojourn was the encounter with the French conductor Walther Straram, who invited Krása as his assistant to Paris and then to Chicago. Krása declined the offer, and instead went to Paris to pursue further studies with Albert Russell. And once again, not even excellent prospects for artistic assertion could surmount Krása's homesickness, and he rushed home to Prague and to his mother, spending only a few months in France.

Despite all the acceptance and success, Krása's life style could be described as a strange mixture of bourgeois and Bohemian. His day started shortly before noon, in the early afternoon he spent a few hours in the theater or giving private lessons to the young ladies from Prague society, and in the late afternoon he went to the office of the German newspaper in Prague, the *Prager Tagblatt*. There he met with the editor-in-chief, Thomas, and several actors, artists, and writers. After a lively debate concerning mainly topical artistic events, he would indulge in at least one game of chess with Thomas, a passion he had inherited from his father and which remained with him during his entire life. The evening would be spent with the Thomas Family or in some nightclub. That he managed to find time for composition is almost incomprehensible.

Obviously, leading such a life, Krása could not produce many works. This was a deplorable waste of talent, since all of Krása's compositions had been performed and favorably accepted, and most of them were also published in Vienna and Paris. In 1926, Krása composed *Five Songs for Voice and Piano*, and it took six years before he came up with the next composition, the cantata *Die Erde ist des Herrn* (The Earth is the Lord's). In the same year, 1932, he finished another major work, the opera *Verlobung im Traum* (Betrothal in a Dream), based on Dostoyevsky's *Uncle's Dream*. The opera was premiered on Prague Radio in March 1933 and staged in the German Theater in May of the same year under the conductor George Szell. Krása received a Czechoslovak State Prize for Composition in 1933 for this work, not a small feat, considering that he was competing against a number of Czech composers.

Hans Krása never gained access into the mainstream of Czech musical life. Perhaps it was a lack of understanding on the side of the Czech musicians, or maybe professional jealousy, deriving from the fact that his works several times represented Czechoslovak musical creativity abroad, even as far as America, where Koussevitzky presented Krása's symphony in a concert of the Boston Symphony Orchestra in Boston in November 1926.

Instead, Krása became associated with Czech artists, writers, and avant-garde theater, in addition to the German authors. It was in these circles where he met Adolf Hoffmeister, a Czech playwright, with whom he collaborated on two different occasions. The year 1935 witnessed not one but two premieres of the same work: Hoffmeister's stage play, *Mládí ve hře* (Youth in the Game), with incidental music by Krása, in the Czech theater D 35,[35] and also the German version of the same piece in the *Kleine Bühne* (Small Stage) in Prague. Krása's music was so successful that one selection, the *Anna Song*, became a hit song for the next several years. Apparently the composer himself was very pleased with the result, because he used the melody as a theme for the *String Quartet "Theme with Variations,"* and also in his *Chamber Music for Cembalo and Seven Instruments,* dedicated to the pianist Frank Pollak,[36] who played the premiere for the Music Section of the Artists Association *Mánes* in Prague, in March 1936.

The second collaboration with Hoffmeister resulted in Krása's last work before his incarceration in Terezín, the children's opera *Brundibár.*

Some publications erroneously attribute to Krása the authorship of the opera *Lysistrata*, based on the ancient play of Aristophanes. Before the war, Krása actually intended to compose this opera with Max Brod, who started to write the German libretto. However, the work did not progress beyond the planning stage, as is evident from a letter sent by Max Brod to K. Sulcová on February 11, 1965: "I started to write for him (Krása) a German text based on Lysistrata. I finished one act. After that, both of us lost interest (Hitler ante portas) and we did not continue in the work." So, the only thing left from the project was an announcement in the newspaper that Krása was working on a new opera.

The tragic events which followed the fateful Munich aggreement caught Krása by surprise and unprepared. His sister, Mitzi, and

[35]D-35 stands for *Divadlo-35* (Theater 1935) and each year the number increased by one, according to the calendar year, i.e. D-36, until D-39, when the operation ceased for political reasons.

[36]Frank Pollak emigrated to Israel before the war and settled in Haifa, changing his name to Frank Pelleg.

brother, Fritz, were abroad, and some of his associates, including Hoffmeister, who did not extend a helping hand, found their way out of Czechoslovakia. After the German invasion, Krása wanted to leave also, but it was too late. Instead, on April 10, 1942, he came to Terezín.

Once he had joined the mainstream of the musical life in the ghetto, Hans Krása turned his attention to composition again. In a little more than two ensuing years, he reconstructed his *Theme with Variations* for string quartet, thus returning for the last time to his most popular tune, the *Anna Song*. Karel Fröhlich played the piece several times with his Terezín String Quartet. It is not known how closely it resembled the original version, since the preserved manuscript contains only the first page, the theme itself. Fröhlich and his associates, Romuald Süssmann and Fred Mark, introduced also the string trio called *Tanz* (Dance), which Krása wrote in Terezín in 1943. Another composition for the same group, the *Passacaglia and Fugue*, remained unperformed. The difficult score was completed on August 7, 1944, less than two months before the departures of the last big transports to Auschwitz.

The last vocal work of Hans Krása was written in Terezín in the spring of 1943. The *Three Songs* for baritone, clarinet, viola, and cello, are interesting for several reasons. Krása had worked with the Czech text only twice in the past, both times when he collaborated with Karel Hoffmeister. And both times he had to deal with inadequate, naive, and even vulgar lyrics. Obviously, the result could not be very satisfying as far as the use of the Czech language is concerned. What makes the *Three Songs* more formidable is the fact that Krása turned his attention once more to his infatuation with French literature, namely the poetry of Arthur Rimbaud, this time in the apt translation of the modern Czech poet Vítězslav Nezval, thus ultimately breaking away from his German ties. Noteworthy also is the much improved use of the Czech language.

The songs prove Krása's composing facility. The first two bear the same completion date, March 2, 1943, and the last one was written on April 7. This makes one wonder how much Krása could have produced during his lifetime, had he spent more time at work. The songs were heard in Terezín several times in 1943 and 1944, but the names of the performing artists are not available, except for the clarinetist, Fritz Weiss.

Besides the previously mentioned new compositions, Krása was ordered by the SS command to produce a new orchestral score of *Brundibár* in Terezín, as mentioned in the previous chapter, and he was working on a concerto for piano and orchestra. It is difficult to say how far he advanced with that composition, since there are no documents on hand.

By the end of September 1944, Hans Krása outlived his usefulness in Terezín. Joyful strains of *Brundibár* were not needed in the ghetto once the committee of the International Red Cross departed, and scenes from the opera have been immortalized on a celluloid strip. On October 17, 1944, he received from the Nazis their customary reward in Auschwitz.

ELEVEN

Viktor Ullmann

O_f all the composers unwillingly residing in Terezín, Viktor Ullmann left the deepest mark on the musical activities there. Thanks to his untiring efforts, musical performances had been presented in the ghetto; thanks to his literary abilities, we can get some idea of the gamut and artistic standards of the musical offerings there; and above all, thanks to his creative powers, the collection of original compositions which sprang to existence in that concentration camp is richer by twenty works of high artistic quality, ranging from songs and chamber music to choral works and even opera.

Ullmann's own autobiographical data are very sketchy, and hardly provide even the basic information. He was born in Těšín (Teschen)—a town on the Moravian-Polish border—on January 1, 1898, son of a high Austrian army officer. Actually, he was of a noble origin, his title being Baron von Tannfels, but he never used it, especially not in order to assert himself as an artist. Although he never mentioned it, one can safely assume that Ullmann received a secondary education in some gymnasium in Vienna, where he spent most of his youth. His numerous writings reveal a vast knowledge of history, literature, and philosophy, besides his main forte, music. His musical studies included piano lessons with Eduard Steuermann

Viktor Ullmann. Drawing by Petr Kien.

and musical theory and composition with Arnold Schoenberg and his students, Dr. Josef Polnauer and Dr. Heinrich Jalowetz. There is no mention of Ullmann's studies of conducting, and yet it was in this field that he made his living for about ten years.

After the war, in 1919, Viktor Ullmann moved to Prague, where he continued his musical studies for a few years while being employed at the New German Theater. The appointment, rather unusual for such a young musician, was attributed to the intervention of Schoenberg himself. He had to be very impressed by Ullmann's talent and capability if he recommended him to his brother-in-law, Alexander Zemlinsky, the musical director of the opera. Ullmann's duties consisted primarily of vocal coaching, but in December 1921, he wielded the baton in the performance of *Bastien and Bastienne*, as he substituted for his superior. Ullmann's conducting activities increased when he was entrusted with the Czech operas of Bedřich Smetana, the field of operetta, and incidental music for the dramatic productions, which he sometimes also composed. Occasionally he conducted the standard repertoire, but only as a substitute. Together with his work at the theater, Ullmann assisted Zemlinsky at the German Male Choral Society in Prague (*Deutscher Männergesangsverein*), for example during the preparation of Schoenberg's *Gurre-Lieder*.

In 1929 Ullmann left Prague to become music director of the opera house in the North Bohemian town of Ústí nad Labem (Aussig). For the first time in his life, he found himself in a position to make his own artistic decisions. He premiered there seven new productions not only from the standard repertoire but also from the contemporary: *Ariadne auf Naxos* by Richard Strauss and *Johny spielt auf* by Ernst Křenek. With such success, it is therefore puzzling that he left Ústí after only a single season. His trail leads to Vienna and Zurich in 1930, but in May of the following year he returned to Czechoslovakia.

Back in Prague, Ullmann's activities moved in a different direction. He gave private music lessons, wrote reviews for the German magazine *Der Auftakt* (The Up-beat), presented lectures, and from time to time collaborated with the music department of Czechoslovak Radio. Unfortunately, all these involvements did not suffice for a comfortable living. Around this time, Ullmann started to organize private music meetings, where new works received first readings or new recordings were listened to and discussed. These meetings continued until the first years of the German occupation, when they acquired even greater importance.

Viktor Ullmann presented himself as composer for the first time in Prague on March 10, 1923, in a concert of the German Association for Literature and Arts (*Literarisch-künstlerischer Verein*). The same organization introduced Ullmann's compositions in the ensuing years, although his creative output was very low. As a matter of fact, from the time he first came to Prague until 1935, he produced only seven complete works. On the last of them, the *Second String Quartet*, he worked for six years.

For some unknown reason, the year 1935 signaled a marked change in Ullmann's artistic life. It was the year when he resumed his studies in composition, this time with Alois Hába at the Prague Conservatory. He graduated two years later with a *Sonata in B♭ Minor* for clarinet and piano in a quarter tone system, the only work in which Ullmann ever ventured into the area of microtones. In 1935 Ullmann also wrote his largest composition up to that time, the opera *Der Sturz des Antichrist* (The Downfall of Antichrist). The three acts were written between June and December of that year to the libretto of the Swiss poet and dramatist Albert Steffen. The cast of nine soloists and chorus is accompanied by an enlarged symphony orchestra. The score has been preserved, but the opera was never performed.

Only once previously, in 1928, did Ullmann attempt to compose an opera. It was *Peer Gynt*, based on the famous drama of Henrik Ibsen. He never finished the work, and the music is not available. Between 1935 and September 1942, when he was sent to Terezín, Ullmann composed a respectable number of pieces, many of which he published privately. Some of them are deposited at the Charles University in Prague, Department of Music History and Theory, others are documented only through reviews and various writings. Noteworthy among the preserved works are the four piano sonatas, a piano concerto, several song cycles, and another opera on a text by Heinrich von Kleist, *Der zerbrochene Krug*, (The Broken Jug). At least ten additional compositions are unaccounted for in view of the existing opus numbers.

From an economic point of view, Ullmann did not fare very well during the last decade preceding the outbreak of the war. In this respect, then, his sojourn in Terezín meant for him a certain release from the daily obligations of making a living. As a former youngest officer in the Austrian army during the First World War, he could also expect preferential treatment in Terezín, and safety from transports leading to the gas chambers. Did he really trust the perfidious Nazis? Apparently not, because he made an earnest effort to leave Czechoslovakia. Unfortunately his friends, Albert Steffen in Switzerland, and Josef Trávnícek-Trauneck, a disciple of Schoenberg residing in South Africa, not only did not help him but advised him to stay in Prague.

Viktor Ullmann came to Terezín with his third wife, Elisabeth, in one of the four transports, which arrived there on September 8, 1942. For a short time he lived very close to his two former wives and one of his sons, who were sent to Terezín several months earlier. Two other children from his second marriage found their way to Sweden and then to England when their parents took advantage of the few transports which the Germans allowed for humanitarian purposes. It happened to be a dubious blessing, because both of the children could not cope with the separation, and spent the rest of their lives in an asylum.

Ullmann was assigned to the *Freizeitgestaltung* as a music critic and organizer of musical rehearsals and practice allotments for the pianists. His light duties enabled him to devote considerable time to preparing and presenting various musical performances, such as concerts of the "Studio for New Music," which possibly fell into the area of his official obligations; but these light duties permitted him, above all, to devote himself to the most concentrated compositional creativity in his life. As if he felt that time was running out, in the period of two years Ullmann completed sixteen known compositions, while another four remained either unfinished or have been partially lost. Many of these were major works, such as three piano sonatas, a string quartet, several song cycles, and the previously described opera, *Der Kaiser von Atlantis*. Of lesser musical importance are his arrangements of Hebrew and Yiddish songs for various choral groups. Still, there is some significance in them. It seems that

First page of Viktor Ullmann's song, *Säerspruch.*

for the first time in his life, Ullmann became aware of his "Jewishness" only in Terezín. Even though he had married three women of his faith, he was never a religious person. Instead, he became a staunch supporter of the anthroposophic movement of Rudolf Steiner, which, in turn, led to the prewar association with Albert Steffen and Alois Hába, both adherents of Steiner's teaching.

Three of the Hebrew choruses were arranged for a boys' choir and dedicated to Ullmann's son, Max. They arose from the composer's untiring interest in youth, which he further demonstrated by giving piano lessons to the adopted son of the Chairman of the Council of Elders, Dr. Epstein, theory lessons to the young violinist Tomás˘ Mandl, and by presentation of original works written in Terezín by young composers, to mention just a few examples.

The first composition of Viktor Ullmann originating in Terezín, in the autumn of 1942, is not a new work. The *Three Songs for Baritone and Piano,* to the poetry of Conrad Ferdinand Meyer, bear the note *"Erneuert* (renewed) *in Theresienstadt."* The prewar version is not in existence, and there is no indication when Ullmann composed it for the first time.

Ullmann's use of opus numbers is misleading because, perhaps overly critical of himself, he destroyed many of his works and rewrote others, years after the completion of the original version; he gave them new numbers or did not number them at all. However, it stands to reason that, with his opus 39, a sonata for violin and piano, Ullmann commenced his Terezín composition period. Only the whole, but undated, violin part was preserved. At the beginning of 1943, a piano was still not easily accessible in the ghetto, while stringed instruments had been thriving for over a year. That could very easily be the reason why Ullmann decided to write his *Third String Quartet* in January 1943 and the song, *Herbst* (Autumn) for voice and string trio. The *Third Quartet* has only one movement, but it is quite extensive and diversified. Ullmann dedicated the score to Professor Emil Utitz. It is not known whether it was ever performed in Terezín.

Ullmann's meeting with his good friend Dr. H. G. Adler resulted in their collaboration on two different occasions. Dr. Adler was an accomplished poet, writer, and musicologist, who could easily fulfill

Ullmann's request for a cycle of twelve short poems, somewhat resembling the Japanese haiku. The poems do not make any reference to the seasons, but their number is based on the number of months. The cycle itself is entitled: *Der Mensch und sein Tag* (The Man and His Day), and Ullmann's score, completed at the beginning of September 1943, calls for a baritone voice and piano. From another song cycle for mezzo soprano and piano, based on four poems of Dr. Adler, only the first two are in existence: *Immer Inmitten* (Always amidst), and *Vor der Ewigkeit* (Before Eternity). It is not known whether Ullmann ever finished all four songs or whether two of them have been lost.

In a number of additional songs and lieder, Ullmann used the poetry of Friedrich Hölderlin, Frank Wedekind, Yiddish texts, German translations of Chinese poems, and even French nursery rhymes. The latter category is represented only by one short song with an English title, *Little Cakewalk*. In this humorous piece, written entirely in French and dedicated to his mother (*"A mon Maman, 27.IX. 1943, Victoire"*),[37] Ullmann made a rare reference to his noble origin He supplemented his signature, at the end of the song, with his otherwise never used title, Baron Tannfels, further adding: "Village du Therese, avec gratulation." Obviously, the song was written in jest, with the note at the repeat sign instructing: "repetition avec humeur jusqu' au fin de siecle" (repeat with humor till the end of time). The *Little Cakewalk* is actually the first song of a cycle called *Chansons des enfants français* (Songs of French children), but once again we do not know whether Ullmann did not complete the intended work or whether the rest of the songs were lost.

Two of the three piano sonatas composed by Ullmann in Terezín have caused considerable confusion. The title of the *Fifth Sonata* had been changed to *First Symphony*, and Ullmann made some notes for orchestration in the piano part, and even wrote a fragment of an orchestral score. The complete version of the sonata has six

---

[37]The French quotation is an exact copy of Ullmann's original with all mistakes in grammar and vocabulary, disclosing the composer's limited knowledge of the language.

movements, while another partial copy contains only the first and third part, skipping the second, the minuet *Totentanz*. The *Fifth Sonata* is in C Major, and, according to Dr. Adler, Ullmann wrote a symphony in D Major in Terezín. That happens to be the tonality of the *Seventh Sonata*, dedicated to Ullmann's children, Max, Jean, and Felice. Ironically, the first page bears the date August 22, 1944—less than two months before he perished in Auschwitz—and Ullmann's limited copyright notice: *"Das Recht der Aufführung bleibt dem Komponisten bei Lebzeiten vorbehalten."* (The performance rights remain reserved to the composer during his lifetime.) The sonata is in five movements, three of them filled with notes for orchestration, ranging from a cembalo and harp to heavy percussions and brass. Considering all preserved documents and testimonies, it may be assumed with reasonable accuracy that the *Seventh Sonata* for piano is actually Ullmann's missing *Symphony in D Major*. The absence of the orchestral score—if he ever produced one—is outweighed by numerous notes for orchestration, which would make it possible to write the score following the composer's intentions.

The most momentous work composed by Viktor Ullmann in Terezín is the opera *Der Kaiser von Atlantis*, described in a previous chapter. It is almost unbelievable that, having written so much music in such a short span of time, Ullmann was working on another opera. Being endowed with literary talent, he wrote his own libretto to a planned opera in two acts, *Joan of Arc*. However, events beyond his control did not permit him to even start on the musical sketches.

To complete the survey of the work of this extraordinary artist, it ought to be said that Ullmann composed in Terezín four cadenzas to the first four piano concertos of Beethoven, and dedicated them to Renée Gärtner-Geiringer. Nonexisting now is the incidental music to the ballads of the French poet François Villon, presented in the dramatization of Irena Dodalová, also a stage director for the occasion. Dr. Jiří Běhal, a lawyer and a talented amateur actor who lost his life later in Kaufering, portrayed the author in a prison scene amid fellow prisoners and prostitutes, reciting and singing Villon's poems in the Czech translation of O. Fischer. Ullmann wrote the music for a violin, a clarinet, a guitar, percussions, and a harmonium, which he also played. For Ullmann, this is the only known case of working with a Czech text; for Irena Dodalová, the entire presentation was an act of protest.[38]

The literary legacy of Viktor Ullmann consists of the twenty-seven musical reviews, the single most important document about the musical activities in the Terezín ghetto, and a diary in the form of poems, *Der fremde Passagier* (The Strange Passenger).

Viktor Ullmann's stay in Terezín came to an abrupt end on October 16, 1944, when he was shipped with his wife Elisabeth to Auschwitz. One week later, his ex-wife Annie and son Max followed; all perished immediately upon arrival.

While all other composers in Terezín left behind only thirty preserved musical scores, Ullmann's bequest comprises twenty extant compositions. And while the others often wrote short pieces for immediate consumption, he followed his own artistic dictates, producing major works of extensive proportions. The remarkable story of how all of Ullmann's music was saved is worthy of recounting.

Upon learning of his departure to the East, Ullmann packed all his belongings for the forthcoming trip. However, the shadows of uncertainty and doubt about his fate after leaving the ghetto changed his mind. So, almost at the last minute, he gave his music and writings to his friend, Dr. Emil Utitz, with the request that he keep them for him and return them after the war. In case Ullmann should not survive, Utitz was instructed to give the material to Dr. H. G. Adler, provided both men would see the liberation. All of this took place under very confusing and frantic circumstances, when 18,500 Terezín inmates were being hauled away to Auschwitz. After the war, Dr. Utitz did meet Dr. Adler and gave him the collection. To Adler's surprise, it also included compositions of Zikmund Schul. Dr. Adler did not stay in Prague very long, only about two years, before he emigrated to England. The combination of the unknown whereabouts of the music, and testimonies of several artists who were unaware of the fact that Ullmann changed his mind about taking the scores with him, resulted in the opinion widely accepted for a long time that the music had been lost. Fortunately, quite the contrary was true.

[38]Information furnished by Tomás Mandl in a letter to the author, July 17, 1979.

TWELVE

Other Composers

Krása, Haas, Ullmann, and Klein were not the only composers active in Terezín. True, they were the most significant ones and the most prolific. Also, they composed music of such quality that it deserves to become part of a standard repertoire purely on its artistic merit rather than for its historic interest. However, there lived a number of people in the Terezín ghetto who wrote compositions of varying value, usually for the needs of the performing artists and ensembles. Their music represents a scope of creativity from aspiring talented young musicians, through professional performers expressing themselves occasionally through smaller forms, to amateurs and students who never got the chance for artistic development. Still, due to the very nature of their music, they became an integral part of the musical life in Terezín.

The first to be mentioned in this category is Zikmund (also spelled Siegmund) Schul, native of Kassel in Germany, born on January 11, 1916. He studied composition with Paul Hindemith in Berlin and came to Prague several years before the Nazi occupation, apparently to find haven from the German persecution in his native land. In the years 1937–38, he resumed his studies with Professor Alois Hába, who became not only his mentor but his benefactor as well. Schul's

Carlo S. Taube. Drawing by Petr Kien.

life in Prague was one of hardship. On the brighter side was his friendship with the family of Rabbi Lieben from the Old-New Synagogue. There he found medieval manuscripts of Hebrew chants, interesting for the use of quarter-tones and sixth-tones, together with other orientalisms. Hába was intrigued by the find and convinced the authorities at the offices of the Jewish community in Prague about the importance of transcribing these manuscripts. The task was entrusted to Schul, who thus found means of livelihood. However, the situation worsened with the German invasion of Czechoslovakia in 1939; the Nazis caught up with Schul in Prague in 1941 and sent him to Terezín on November 11 of that year.

The compositional endeavors of Zikmund Schul did not cease with his incarceration. Quite the contrary, as early as December 22, 1941, he wrote the first of the *Two Chassidic Dances* for viola and cello, op. 15, and he completed the second shortly after, on January 2 of the following year. Schul's version of a three-part boys' chorus, *Ki tavoa al-haerez* (When you will go to the land), based on an old Hebrew song, is dated January 30, 1942, and the ensuing arrangement of Grünfeld's melody for a string quartet, *Uv'tzeil K'nofecho* (In the Shadow of Your Wings), was finished less than a week later, on February 4. It should be mentioned that all of these compositions are very short and are written for not more than four voices.

One can only theorize about whether Schul stopped composing for the next ten months or whether his subsequent works have been lost. The final fugue from a *Cantata Judaica*, a one-page fragment for a male chorus with a short cantorial tenor solo, was dated "Ghetto Theresienopolis, 4. XII. 1942." It is Schul's only other composition from Terezín provided with an opus number, which is, strangely enough, thirteen. That could indicate that the composer reconstructed a previously written larger work for some special occasion or group, not even in its entirety.

The aforementioned compositions reveal Zikmund Schul's deep interest in Hebraic thematic and religious mysticism. Hebrew chant was the main source from which he drew inspiration for his music. The only composition not showing the strong Hebraic character is the song *Schicksal* (Fate), for alto, flute, viola, and cello. Schul wrote it to the text of H. Schläger, on May 17, 1943, approximately six months after the arrival of Viktor Ullmann in Terezín. Schul befriended the well known composer and undoubtedly welcomed or even solicited his advice.

The most extensive and last finished work of Zikmund Schul, the *Duo for Violin and Viola,* was composed between March 22 and May 28, 1943. More than twenty pages of the original score contain the last three movements and a fragment of the first one. Unfortunately, it is the entire beginning, seventy-four measures to be exact, which are missing, and would therefore be difficult to reconstruct.

Schul's talent was not limited to music. In Terezín he also wrote several poems, revealing the mental torment and anguish imposed on him by the incarceration. His very heavy-hearted nature, combined with the lack of will to live under the severe conditions, resulted in the deterioration of his mental and physical health. His creative activity came to a standstill during the last year of his life, and he finally succumbed to tuberculosis in Terezín on June 20, 1944.

In direct contrast to the sickly Schul, the ebullient Karel Berman always found new avenues for his irrepressible talent. Born in Jindřichův Hradec (Bohemia), on April 14, 1919, he learned there the fundamentals of music before entering the voice class of the Prague Conservatory in 1938. Unfortunately, two years later, in 1940, his studies were forcibly interrupted, and the following year he started his odyssey of the concentration camps.

As a versatile musician, Berman took part in all kinds of musical activities in Terezín as organizer, singer, conductor, stage director, and pianist. It is therefore not surprising that he ventured also into the field of composition. In an outburst of creativity, in March and April of 1944, he wrote three songs for high voice and piano, and an exhilarating cycle of four songs for basso and piano, called *Poupata* (The Rosebuds), and a melancholy suite for piano, named, appropriately, *Terezín.* Intermingled, according to the composer's instructions, the latter two pieces effectively change the mood, thus expressing vividly the uncertainty of everyday life in the ghetto. The whereabouts of Berman's orchestral march is not known, the author did not consider it worthwhile to rewrite this incidental piece of music after his liberation.

Fate was not very kind to the pianist and composer Carlo S. Taube, born on July 4, 1897 in Galizien. To prepare himself for a career as piano virtuoso, he studied for several years with Ferruccio Busoni in Vienna. However, instead of embarking on a solo career, economic pressures forced him to search for a means of livelihood playing in the cafés and nightclubs, first in Vienna and later in Brno and Prague. Only after his arrival in Terezín, where he came with his wife Erika and their child in December 1941, did Taube's career seemingly go on an upswing. Relieved of daily obligations to provide for his family, he turned his energy and his ambition to musical activities which had been inaccessible to him up to this time. He presented several piano recitals, with pretentious programs, consisting of works by Beethoven, Brahms, Schumann, Liszt, and Chopin, to more or less captive audiences. Despite his unquestionable talent, he was not always very successful, as is evident from a review by Viktor Ullmann; the latter attributed to Taube a great talent and innate prerequisites but felt that Taube had to make a decision concerning which way he really wanted to proceed. Besides playing the piano, Taube tried to pursue the path of conductor and composer.

Being experienced in writing only short pieces, Taube undertook a pompous project in Terezín, which he entitled *The Terezín Symphony*. The score of this work was not preserved, and one can only guess at the quality and scope of the music. The existence of the music and the premiere performance were witnessed by Dr. H. G. Adler, whose opinion of the work was less than laudatory, and Arnošt Weiss, who had the following recollection in his memoirs:

Carlo Taube had completed the composition of his *Terezín Symphony* and invited me to a private premiere in the prayer room of the Magdeburg barracks. A small string orchestra sat at their stands on the podium and behind them stood four men with accordions that substituted for brass and woodwinds and for which some parts had to be rewritten because of the deadness of their tone. Greeted heartily by the full hall, the composer took his place at the conductor's stand for the first orchestral concert in the ghetto. Not much remains in my memory from the first two movements that characterized the milieu

125

First page of Carlo Taube's lullaby, *Ein Jüdisches Kind.*

with Jewish and Slavic themes. But the third movement had a shattering effect on the listeners. Mrs. Erika Taube, the wife of the composer, recited in a moving way, with a pianissimo obligato from the orchestra, a lullaby of a Jewish mother, which she had composed. There followed a turbulent finale in which the first four bars of *Deutschland über Alles* were repeated over and over again out in more and more wrathful spasms, until the last outcry... *"Deutschland, Deutschland"*... did not continue to *"über Alles,"* but died out in a terrible dissonance. Everyone had understood and a storm of applause expressed thanks to Carlo and Erika Taube and all the musicians. Naturally a work of this sort could not be performed officially and it is distressing that this unique cultural document was not passed on to us."[39]

Arnošt Weiss wrote his reminiscence twenty years after the liberation. The accuracy of his memory is questionable, since there is a document resembling his story closely, with a few minor differences. According to it, a program took place in the "Cavalier" barracks on May 3, 1942, called *Ghetto Lullaby*, by Carlo Taube in the framework of his *Ghetto Suite* for orchestra and alto voice.

Equally nonexistent are three short pieces of Carlo Taube for violin and piano, *Poem, Caprice,* and *Meditation,* which were introduced to the Terezín audiences by Karel Fröhlich. The only souvenir of Taube and his wife is a lullaby for soprano and piano, *Ein Jüdisches Kind* (A Jewish Child), composed on November 4, 1942, and apparently not the same as the lullaby from the symphony. The song is a moving expression of parents' love for their child, unable to provide him with a proper home. Musically it shows a strong affinity to Hebraic chant combined with elements of popular music of the prewar style. "The Jewish Child" never found his homeland, losing his life, together with his parents, in the Auschwitz gas chambers around October 11, 1944.

In order to enrich their repertoire, not one but two members of the Ledeč Quartet wrote shorter pieces for their ensemble. The first one was the leader of the group, Egon Ledeč. This former associate

[39]Reprinted with permission from the book *Terezín.*

127

concertmaster of the Czech Philharmonic was born in Kostelec nad Orlicí, Bohemia, on March 16, 1889. He studied violin at the Prague Conservatory and started concertizing in Czech towns and cities as a teenager. In 1908 he joined the Czech Philharmonic; after the First World War he played in several Slovak orchestras; and finally, in 1926, he rejoined the Czech Philharmonic as associate concertmaster. He remained in this function until the German occupation of Czechoslovakia and his subsequent imprisonment in Terezín. During all those years, Ledeč was active as a soloist and chamber music player as well as composer of semiclassical pieces, waltzes, marches, small compositions for violin and piano, etc. The only known and preserved work from his stay in Terezín is a charming little salon piece with luscious melodies and piquant harmonies, named *Gavotte*. Ledeč wrote it for his string quartet in December 1942. Less than two years later, on October 16, 1944, he boarded a cattle car heading for Auschwitz.

Very little is known about the violist of the Ledeč Quartet, Viktor Kohn. He lived in the old historical section of Prague, Malá Strana (Lesser Town), and had a reputation as an excellent violist. Kohn came to Terezín with his brother, Paul Kohn, who had for some time played cello in the quartet of Egon Ledeč, besides being a very good flutist. According to some survivors, Viktor Kohn died in Terezín in his early forties. Equally scarce is any information about his composing activities, since his entire "estate" consists of a single piece, which he wrote in Terezín on December 4, 1942. It is a *Praeludium* for a string quartet, dedicated to Kohn's friends and members of the Council of Elders, Jakob Edelstein and Otto Zucker. This modernistically conceived composition is based on three notes, E-D-E, paying homage to EDElstein. It bears the opus number 12-a, thus indicating that Kohn had written music before his arrival in Terezín, and possibly at least opus 12-b, while there. The probability of recovering any of Viktor Kohn's compositions is very remote, and it can be assumed that their style and character will remain a mystery.

One of the luckier musicians who survived the ordeal of Terezín and Auschwitz was František Domažlický. A native of Prague born on May 13, 1913, he came to Terezín in 1941 as an amateur violinist and trumpet player. In this capacity he also participated as performer of light music in the Terezín "café." Although he did not willingly destroy them, Domažlický dismissed several pieces which he composed in the ghetto as not worthy of preservation. Actually, only one original score remains in existence, a song for a male chorus, *Píseň máje* (The May Song). It is a sentimental piece of music, similar to the popular songs which Domažlický wrote before the war, with lyrics provided by the composer himself. Another composition for a male quartet and alto solo, *Sterne* (Stars), was dedicated to Hedda Grab-Kernmayr, who sang the premiere on September 23, 1942 in the "Magdeburg" barracks. Nothing is known about the piece, of which even the composer does not have any recollection. Finally, the third documented work, a little encore piece for a string quartet, *Lied ohne Worte* (Song without Words), had been preserved at least in the author's head if not on paper. After the war, Domažlický rewrote it with a few imperceptible changes for a whole string orchestra.

Ilse Weber belongs in a category of complete amateurs. She was born in Vítkovice in northern Moravia on January 11, 1903, but her married life was spent in Prague. As a mother of two young sons, she wrote for them three children's books with short stories and fairytales. Before they went to Terezín in 1942 with their younger son, Tommy, the Webers managed to send their older boy, Hanuš, to Sweden, thus relieving him of all the afflictions of the concentration camps. Ilse Weber worked in Terezín as a head nurse in the children's ward; as such, she had a good chance of staying there until the end of the war.

The sensitive mind of Ilse Weber absorbed all the misery and longing caused by the sojourn in the ghetto, and she put her impressions into roughly one hundred German and Czech poems, perhaps not very artistic but nevertheless very eloquent and moving. Several of these poems she put to music, thus creating songs with simple melodies and simple piano accompaniment, sometimes bordering on crudeness. The most effective of them is *Ich wandre durch Theresienstadt*:

> I wander through Theresienstadt,
> My heart a lump of lead.

Weber family. Photo taken in 1939.
From left to right: Ilse, Tommy, Hanuš, Vilém.

The road all of a sudden ends,
Near where the fortress stands.

There, on the bridge, I stop and gaze
Across the valley below.
I'd like so much to walk beyond,
To go back home just now.

"Home," so beautiful a word,
My heart cries out aloud.
They took my home away from me,
And now I am without.

I turn away, bewildered, tired,
My heart is torn with pain.
Theresienstadt, Theresienstadt,
When will the suffering end, and when
Will we be free again?

Ilse Weber's suffering ended, but without the yearned-for freedom. When her husband, Vilém, was summoned for transport to the East in the fall of 1944, she volunteered to accompany him with Tommy. Her wish not to break up the family resulted in the execution of Ilse and her son in Auschwitz, while her husband survived her by some thirty years.

It is almost a miracle how many works of art created in Terezín have been preserved for posterity, be it drawings and paintings, poetry, or musical scores. However, many others have been destroyed or lost, and we know about them only from various documents or testimonies of survivors, sometimes, ironically, speaking about themselves.

One such case is that of Dr. Karel Reiner. The son of a cantor, he was born in Žatec, Bohemia, on June 27, 1910. Although he graduated from the Charles University in Prague as Doctor of Law, since his youth Reiner had pursued musical studies of piano and composition, the latter at the Master School in Prague with Josef Suk and later with Alois Hába in his department of microtones. As a pianist, Reiner made his debut in 1926, and he continued in a public career as a recitalist and much sought after accompanist until the

Nazi occupation. For the next few years he worked for the Jewish Community office in Prague as organizer of musical activities; in 1943 he was deported to Terezín.

As a composer, Karel Reiner had to his credit a long line of works for orchestra, choruses, piano, chamber music, and songs, and, as a collaborator with the avant-garde theater D-35 and radio in Prague, incidental music to a number of dramatic productions. It was mainly in this vein that he resumed composition in the Terezín ghetto.

It has to be understood that among many cultural activities in Terezín, music was only one of several facets of artistic expression. Another very important one was the theater, so extensive that it had several branches: Czech, German, Jewish, and children's, including puppets and marionettes. Dramas and comedies of old masters took turns with plays of questionable quality, folk plays, and works that sprang into existence in the ghetto itself. On rare occasions, music was utilized for regular drama, with the experienced Karel Reiner ready to help out. He wrote and performed on the piano incidental music to the comedy of Edmund Rostand, *The Romancers*, staged by Vlasta Schönová in the "Hamburg" barracks, and in 1944 he composed musical background for a gala production of the Czech play, *Švanda, the Bagpiper*, by Josef Kajetán Tyl, for a small orchestra. As ill luck would have it, the big transports in the fall of 1944 not only prevented the realization of these plans but also caused the loss of all of Reiner's musical material.

The most successful presentation with Reiner's incidental music, written for a small instrumental ensemble and voices, was the folk play *Esther* in the dramatization of E. F. Burian, the director of theater D-35. The story itself is taken from the Old Testament and describes the deliverance of the Jews from annihilation through the intervention of Queen Esther. The story had a special significance for Jews imprisoned in the concentration camp, and it is therefore rather surprising that the presentation met with all kinds of objections from various factions in Terezín, which tried to ascribe to the work some hidden ideological, religious, or political (communist) meaning, and at the same time to question its originality and artistic content. Karel Reiner composed the music, suitable to the folk style of the drama. Hans Jochowitz conducted the orchestra, while Norbert

(Nora) Fried[40] directed the play, using costumes designed by František Zelenka. The score was not preserved, but after the war some of the surviving actors remembered several songs and tunes, and the composer transcribed them without any accompaniment or arrangement, thus leaving them virtually useless.

Dr. Reiner could not devote much time to composition in Terezín. He did not belong to the *Freizeitgestaltung*. He worked for children's welfare, and from time to time played piano for the musical performances. He also reintroduced his cycle of nursery rhymes *Květovaný kůň* (The Flower Horse), written in 1942 to the text of Nora Fried and performed previously in one of the Jewish orphanages in Prague.

To satisfy his artistic needs and ambitions, Reiner resumed in Terezín his interrupted work on a cycle of choruses in the sixth-tone system, based on the poetry of Christian Morgenstern, in the Czech translation of Emil A. Saudek. Of course, this very modernistic music was not meant for the performances in the ghetto.

To complete the picture of the musical creative output in Terezín, one should at least mention a few additional names, although other information is almost nonexistent. Heinz Alt, a talented youngster, probably in his teens, hailed from the Moravian city of Ostrava. His *Six Miniatures* for piano, composed in Terezín, received its premiere there during the second concert of the "Studio for New Music." He also wrote several songs, but the whereabouts of his compositions are unknown. Alt survived Terezín and Auschwitz, only to die shortly before the liberation in the concentration camp Kauffering.

Even scarcer is the documentation concerning Antonín Roubíček, possibly another student, whose *Elegy* for piano was found after the war, and M. Kron (even his complete first name is not available), presumably a dilettante, who wrote a *Rhapsody* for piano, which was similarly preserved. Both Roubíček and Kron perished in Auschwitz.

Finally, there is a notebook in the Terezín archives with forty-eight children's pieces for piano. Various styles and quality indicate that they were written by different people, but their purpose is not clear. Were they written by children or by grown-ups for children's instruction? Will anyone ever know?

[40]After the war he changed the spelling to Frýd.

G.VERDI:

REQUIEM

DIRIGENT: RAFAEL SCHÄCHTER

SOLI:

G. BORGER	SOPRAN
H. ARANSON LINDT	MEZZO-SOPRAN
D. GRÜNFELD	TENOR
K. BERMANN	BASS

GEMISCHTER CHOR

AM KLAVIER: GIDEON KLEIN

Poster for *Requiem* by Giuseppe Verdi.

THIRTEEN

"Requiem Aeternam
Dona Eis Domine..."

Lo! The book exactly worded,
Wherein all hath been recorded.
Thence shall judgment be awarded.
When the judge his seat attaineth
And each hidden deed arraineth,
Nothing unavenged remaineth.

(From the sequence *"Dies Iae"*)

E xcept for symphonic music,
obviously impossible in the absence of a full symphony orchestra,
no facet of the musical repertoire remained unheeded in Terezín.
Thus the inhabitants had the opportunity to attend a number of
performances in the field of oratorio and cantata. The conductor,
Karl Fischer, was responsible for the presentation of Haydn's *The
Creation* and Mendelssohn's *Elijah*, while Rafael Schächter added to
his credit Verdi's magnificent *Requiem* and the cantata *The Czech Song*
by Bedřich Smetana.

135

```
M U S I K
    Programm für die Zeit vom 14. bis 20.2.1944.
Montag, den 14.2.1944
    Rathausg.19       18        Klaviertrio (W.Lederer,H.Taussig,
                                P.Kohn) (Kart.vom 12.2.1944)
    Wallstr.8/16      18        Taube-Orchester(Konzertmeister
                                Fröhlich) (Karten-Geld)


Dienstag, den 15.2.1944
    Hauptstr.2/241    17        "Tosca",Leit.F.E.Klein(K.Geld)
    Rathausg.19       17.30     J.Haydn:"Schöpfung",Leit.K.Fisch
                                (Kart.Geld)

Mittwoch, den 16.2.1944
    Rathausg.19       18        Bach-Konzert Edith Steiner-Kraus
                                (Kart.Geld)

Donnerstag, den 17.2.1944
    Hauptstr.2/241    18        Klavierquartette Brahms,Dvořák
    Rathausg.19                 (Gid.Klein, K.Fröhlich, R.Süss-
                                mann F.Mark) (Kart.Geld)

Freitag, den 18.2.1944
    Rathausg.19       13        Chopin-Abend Carlo S.Taube(K.Gel.

Samstag, den 19.2.1944
    Hauptstr.2/241    15.30     Die Fledermaus,Operette von Jo-
                                hann Strauss,Leit.Hans Hofer.
    Rathausg.19       18        Liederabend H.Grab-Kerumayer, am
                                Klavier Dr.K.Reiner (Kart.Geld)
    Wallstr.8/16      19        V.Kohn u.sein Orchester(Kart.Gel.

Sonntag, den 20.2.1944
    Hauptstr.2/241    10.30     Taube-Orchester(Kart.Geld)
    Hauptstr.2/241    16.30     "Die Fledermaus",Operette von Jo-
                                hann Strauss,Leit.Hans Hofer(KG)
    Rathausg.19       17.30     G.Verdi:Requiem.Leit.R.Schächter
                                (Kart.Geld)
```

Program of the Freizeitgestaltung for the
week of February 14th to 20th, 1944.

Although all four presentations are well documented through reviews by Viktor Ullmann, posters, weekly programs of the *Freizeitgestaltung*, and reminiscences of the survivors, there are several details not completely explained. The first concerns the exact days of the premieres, then the number of performances, and to some extent even the names of the participating artists.

As valuable as they are, Ullmann's reviews do not mention the dates, and only on occasion do they indicate the approximate time. Similarly, the posters are without dates. Only a few available weekly schedules give exact information about a performance without, however, mentioning whether it is a premiere or a reprise.

From the fact that one of the performances of the oratorio *Die Schöpfung* (The Creation) took place on February 15, 1944, we can safely deduce that Karl Fischer prepared it sometime in the winter of 1943–44. The poster made for this occasion mentions the names of soloists as Fried (apparently a misspelling of Karel Freund) in the part of Raphael and Adam, (Gertrude) Borger as Gabriel or Eve, and (Machiel) Gobets as Uriel. The mixed choir was accompanied by Renée Gärtner-Geiringer on the piano.

In his review, Ullmann first expressed his not exactly flattering opinion about the work itself, but he praised the performers this way:

> The choruses were, therefore, also the best and the purest joy of our Terezín performance, thanks to the efforts of Karl Fischer, who, as an excellent chorus master, held his youthfully fresh and enthusiastic chorus firmly in his hand. Also the soloists gave their best, headed by Mrs. Kohn-Schlesskov, who is noticed as an experienced oratorio singer, and whose fine coloratura voice was nicely appreciated in the aria *"Auf starkem Fittig."* Mr. Goldring made his debut as an oratorio singer, and he familiarized himself astonishingly fast with the style; his supple tenor offers him for that all advantages, and the aria, *"Mit Würd' und Hoheit angetan ... ,"* succeeded exquisitely. Mr. Freund still needs for his nice endowment a voice teacher; however, all in all he discharged his difficult task honorably. Mrs. Gärtner-Geiringer did not let us miss the absence of an orchestral accompaniment."

The different names of the soloists indicate that Fischer had at his disposal a double cast for multiple performances. The basso part was also sung on two occasions by Bedřich (Wolfgang) Borges, an engineer by profession but an excellent amateur singer. Such an arrangement was necessitated by the fact that often two or more simultaneous musical presentations took place at different locations in Terezín.

During the summer of 1944, Karl Fischer scored another triumph with Mendelssohn's oratorio *Elijah*. This time he chose for his soloists the soprano Gertude Borger, alto Hilde Aronson-Lindt, tenor Michel (also spelled Machiel) Gobets, and basso Walter Windholz as Elijah. Mrs. Kohn-Schlesskov sang a little solo, this time as a member of the chorus, which numbered about eighty people. Instead of the orchestral accompaniment, Dr. Karel Reiner with Mrs. Bach-Fischer played on two upright pianos. Once again, Fischer received critical acclaim from Viktor Ullmann, and the repeats were scheduled until October 1, 1944. Whether the last performance actually took place is not known, since it was after the initiation of the big transports to Auschwitz on September 28. In one of the productions, Borges substituted for Windholz in the role of Elijah.

In the occupied Czech territories, the year 1944 marked a double anniversary of Bedřich Smetana, the founder of modern Czech music. On the second of March, 120 years had elapsed since his birth, and on May 12, six decades since his passing away. During the year, every note written by this beloved composer came to life in public performances, with the exception of the banned patriotic operas, *Libuše* and *The Brandenburgs in Bohemia*. As a result of an appeal to the public, even some of Smetana's music hitherto unknown had been discovered and presented.

Such an occasion could not go unnoticed in Terezín, where the musical life was just about at its peak. The initiator of many musical events, Rafael Schächter, presented a vocal concert devoted entirely to Smetana's compositions in the summer of that year in the Sokolovna hall. In the first half, Walter Windholz sang the *Evening Songs* with Karel Berman at the piano, and the male and female choruses rendered three selections. The *opus maximum* followed after the intermission in the form of the cantata *The Czech Song* in

Schächter's "swinging, lively, dynamically and rhythmically satisfying and well molded performance." Dr. Karel Reiner joined Karel Berman in the accompaniment at the second piano.

Finally, there was the much heralded and perhaps even more disputed and criticized presentation of the *Requiem* by Giuseppe Verdi. In his monumental book *Theresienstadt 1941–45*, Dr. H. G. Adler, himself a musicologist of stature, considered it a "bad blunder," while Josef Bor wrote on the same subject a complete novel, *The Terezín Requiem*, in which he praised Schächter's undertaking.

In order to explain why Schächter had chosen this particular composition for a performance in a Jewish concentration camp, one has to understand several factors. A Requiem is, of course, a Roman Catholic mass for the dead. It has been set to music by a number of great and lesser composers. Verdi's version belongs, without any doubt, to the most elite. However, it was not composed for liturgical use, and its style suggests rather that in this work Verdi wrote one of his most beautiful operas. Schächter's predilection for opera is evident from his previous presentations, and since most of the operas in Terezín were performed only in a concert form, the choice of an oratorio should not be surprising.

Although the Jewish community in Prague had existed for more than a thousand years, Czech Jewry before 1939 was in the vast majority not religious. Jews were, first of all, ardent citizens of the young Czechoslovak Republic, even though many of them spoke German, which was one of the autonomous languages. They assimilated to their environment to such a degree that they celebrated—not religiously—Christmas and Easter. Any kind of artistic endeavor would not offend them. Therefore, *Requiem* in Terezín. Or was there some other reason?

The history of the *Terezín Requiem* is as tragic as it is ironic. Rafael Schächter started to pursue the idea of performing Verdi's *Requiem* sometime in the middle of 1943. By September of that year he assembled four outstanding soloists: Marion Podolier, Hilde Aronson-Lindt, David Grünfeld, and Karel Berman, and a chorus of some 150 singers. (The preserved poster gives the name of the soprano as Gertrude Borger, intimating that she substituted for Podolier on some occasion.) Instead of an orchestra, the accompaniment was provided on the piano, played alternately by Gideon Klein and Tella Polák.[41] The first performance was successfully launched, but the repetition was not realized, because a transport to the East virtually wiped out the entire chorus. (It was most probably the transport to the "Terezín Family Camp" in Auschwitz, on September 6, 1943.) Schächter did not despair. He assembled a new chorus of approximately the same size and eventually presented a second performance. Once again a crushing blow, in the form of another *Osttransport* (Eastern transport), demolished the ensemble. The Sisyphean task started all over, and finally, with the third group, but the same soloists, Schächter gave about fifteen performances.

One can comprehend the success of Verdi's *Requiem* in Terezín by reading what Viktor Ullmann had to say about its presentation in his *Belated Glosses to Verdi's "Requiem"*:

> Yesterday's performance was already one of the so and so many repeats, and one should, therefore, say nothing more about the technical aspect. However, in this case it would appear correct to emphasize once more that Rafael Schächter, to whom the Terezín musical life is indebted for so many stimulations and artistic deeds, delivered a performance of a big-city standard. Growing beyond the technical aspect, Schächter shapes the above discussed spirit of the work, with economical but conjuring gestures. The chorus not only sings precisely but also is dynamically well controlled. The soloists stand to the conductor's side, and in the shining soprano of Podolier— especially in the higher register—the all around warm voice of Aronson-Lindt, the blooming tenor of Grünfeld, and the dark, beautiful and deep basso of Berman, they unite in a bel canto collaboration fascinating the listeners. And who could write better for human voices than Verdi? Why does everything by Verdi sound, while by countless other Masters the human voice does not come to

---

[41]All previous publications mention the name of the second pianist as Edith Steiner Kraus. However, she corrected this allegation in a taped interview with the author on December 29, 1976, in Tel-Aviv.

sounding, but instead gasps like a fish on a dry beach while the rhythmic declamation chops the most beautiful melodies . . . ?

Thankfully we acknowledge the marvelous performance with Gideon Klein at the piano, and we hope that once we will hear on the operatic stage Verdi's true legacy, the incomparable *Falstaff*, which, as wisdom's ultimate conclusion, proclaims in the Master's last and most successful fugue: "All is fun on Earth."

Repeat performances of Verdi's *Requiem* continued well into 1944, and at one point the Nazis ordered Schächter to give a gala performance for the Committee of the International Red Cross, hosted by Adolf Eichmann, during their visit to Terezín. Schächter obliged very gladly, and here the criticism of his doing so attains its high point. Was it a defeatist attitude to present in front of the visitors a chant for the dead—his own condemned confreres—for the enjoyment of their oppressors? Hardly! Instead, it was Schächter's last demonstration of defiance. Under his baton, the condemned sang the *Requiem* for their condemners and their damned Third Reich![42]

"Dies irae, dies illa. . . . "

[42]It should be noted and emphasized that Josef Bor's book, *The Terezín Requiem,* is not an actual account of the history, but a novel, full of melodramatic episodes, based vaguely on the actual performance in the actual surroundings.

Karel Švenk.

FOURTEEN

The Light Muse in Terezín

The voluminous presentations of serious music in Terezín could indicate a neglecting of the Light Muse. However, nothing would be further from the truth than such an assumption. As mentioned in one of the preceding chapters, early in 1942 Karel Švenk presented the first all-male cabaret, called *The Lost Food Card,* for the men living in the "Sudeten" barracks. Besides being amusing, the cabaret had a more important mission: to strengthen the morale of the prisoners. This it achieved above all through the final march which soon became known as the Terezín anthem. Švenk wrote the text as well as the music, and, besides being producer and director, he participated in the performance as actor.

His next variety show, *Long Live Life,* was more complex in its structure, aiming at contemporary social problems. Once again, Švenk deployed all his talents. A sad clown with extremely expressive eyes, he reminded one to some extent of Buster Keaton.

AŤ ŽIJE ŽIVOT
Revue
aneb tanec kolem kostry

napsal:
režie:
hudba:

Karel Švenk

výprava: Dolfi Aussenberg
tance nastudovala: Kamila Rosenbaumova

hrají:

Beck - Bejček	Masárková
Becková Hanna	Pollaková
Bergmann	Popper
Bermann Karel	Pötschauová
Borges	Rosenbaumová Kamila
Dr. Brammer	Siemens
Eckstein Luděk	Spitz
Eckstein Zdeněk	Schönová Vava
Glaserová	Schönová Marie
Goldschmidt	Sušický
Grábová - Kernmeyerová	Steiner
Kraus Cesar	Straussová
Kraus Karel	Švenk Karel
Kavan Karel	Neuschul

Schlieserová, Töpfer Otto, Zajlais.

Poster for Švenk's cabaret, *Long Live Life*.

His incessant work made him a Terezín hero. For his second cabaret Švenk used a number of songs he had composed for his theatrical productions before the war. The high artistic level of the production was vouched for by the participation of such artists as Karel Berman, Hedda Grab-Kernmayr, Kamila Rosenbaum, and Švenk himself. Although *Long Live Life* did not deal directly with problems concerning the life in Terezín, its optimistic songs were uplifting the morale of his audiences.

Of greatest importance was Švenk's third cabaret, *The Last Cyclist*. In this allegory, in which the cyclists representing Jews were targets of persecution by the fools-Nazis, the author did not leave anybody in doubt about his message. For that reason only the open dress rehearsal took place, and the play was immediately forbidden by the Council of Elders. Subsequently, Švenk put together several more or less improvised shows, but they reached neither the quality nor the response of the previous ones. In September, 1944, Karel Švenk made the journey to Auschwitz, but about a month later, he was selected to go as a laborer to a factory in Menselwitz near Leipzig. The heavy work, long hours and insufficient food caused a rapid deterioration of this already weakened health and he passed away in the first week of April, 1945. Only six chansons from his Terezín output have been preserved.

The success of Švenk's cabaret prompted actors Josef Lustig and Jiří Spitz, together with the lyricist František Kowanitz and the set designer Ota Neumann, to follow in his footsteps and form an ensemble modeled rather closely after the Liberated Theater (*Osvobozené divadlo*) in Prague. The similarity did not stop with two main actors, like Voskovec and Werich. It even included the very popular songs of Jaroslav Ježek from the same theater, with topical lyrics of Kowanitz, pertaining to the new situation.[43]

The original Švenk's cabaret could be performed only in the men's barracks. About two months later, the women in the

---

[43]Voskovec, Werich, and Ježek lived during the war in the United States. Ježek died in New York on New Year's Day, 1942; Jan Werich returned after the war to Czechoslovakia; and George Voskovec pursued a successful career in American theater and television.

"Dresden" barracks decided to begin their own "feminine" culture, and they entrusted one of the prisoners, Jana Šedová, with the organization of their new cabaret. Šedová found herself in a quite precarious position, never having even seen a cabaret, let alone participating in one. However, the hunger for a little laughter was so strong that she put together several shows, which were accepted with great gratitude. These amateurish productions did not last long, because, after some time, the gates of the barracks opened, and people could attend cultural activities of their own choice, thus enabling the women to see and also participate in the more sophisticated productions.

Months later, after the initial cabarets of Karel Švenk took place, at a time when more German-speaking Jews came to Terezín, Hans Hofer started his programs with a group of German actors. Soon a number of similar ensembles came into existence under the leadership of Egon Thorn, Boby Morgan, Kurt Gerron, and others. Their activities mushroomed all over the ghetto, mainly because such programs were easy to assemble, and with small groups the show could move from one attic to another and be performed in modest accomodations for limited audiences.

Early in 1944, a new transport arrived from the concentration camp Westerbork in Holland, and with it again several artists, musicians, and actors. As an indirect result, the most ambitious and successful cabaret came into being. The *Lagerkommant*—or, as he preferred to be called, "Leader of the Terezín Administration" (*Dienststelle*)—*Obersturmführer* Karl Rahm ordered the famous and even in Terezín respected movie actor and director, Kurt Gerron, to prepare a German cabaret. Gerron was well known for his similar prewar productions in Berlin, and he achieved fame for his starring role with Marlene Dietrich in the movie *The Blue Angel*. A few years before the outbreak of the war, he sought refuge in the Netherlands. This sanctuary proved not to be very safe when the Nazis invaded that country on May 10, 1940. As in Czechoslovakia, the Jews became subject to the "Jewish laws" and were banned from public life. For a period of time, they had their own theater, not accessible to the "Aryans." It was in this place that Kurt Gerron met an eminent jazz pianist, Martin Roman, who had left Germany earlier, in 1933. A congenial collaboration in the theater followed, only to be discontinued by their incarceration in the concentration camp. Roman went to Vught and Westerbork, and in January 1944 he arrived in Terezín in the same transport as Gerron. There they were reunited in what turned out to be their last joint venture: the cabaret *Karussell* and the propaganda movie *Der Führer schenkt den Juden eine Stadt* (The Führer donates a town to the Jews). This is how Roman describes his meeting with Gerron in Terezín:

> In Terezín one day I got a message to come to the Jewish Burgermeister (Mayor, Elder) Dr. Eppstein.... Anyway, Eppstein said:
>
> "Mr. Roman, why did you never tell me that you are such a fabulous musician?"
>
> I said: "Nobody asked me, sir."
>
> "Do you know this man?"
>
> "Kurt! Kurt Gerron!"
>
> He (Gerron) said: "Martin, Commander Rahm heard that I am here, and he knew me from one of my films, and he said: 'Mr. Gerron, I am honored to meet you.' And he asked me to organize a cabaret and also do the music. I said: 'I have my own arranger and—'
>
> "Where is he? Where is he?"
>
> So, he told me, and from that moment I was released and I did not have to work on the street anymore, and then ... we had a performance, which Rahm attended, and all the German SS society came, there were some Jews invited, and the musicians all knew that.
>
> And Commander Rahm said to the musicians: "Now I show you what *Kunst* (art) is. I have here some Germans, not Czechs, you know. Some Germans."
>
> And Kurt sang, and another guy, Hermann Feiner—he was a great cabaret performer, also a serious actor—he had some chansons which I knew, of course, and I accompanied them from that moment on.[44]

The text of Gerron's *Karussell* was written by Manfred Greiffenhagen and Dr. Leo Strauss, and the show was properly staged on sets by

---

[44]Transcribed from a taped interview with the author on September 8, 1978, in Emerson, New Jersey.

architect František Zelenka. The outstanding cast was headed by Gerron himself, the fine Netherland tenor Machiel Gobets, soprano Anne Frey, and, according to Roman, Hermann Scheiner, whose name, however, does not appear on the preserved poster. The cabaret was very successful not only with the Jewish prisoners but with their Nazi keepers as well. Gerron enjoyed a great reputation in Germany before the war, and it followed him even behind the gates of the concentration camp, where he sustained the admiration of the SS.

Karussell, like all other German cabarets in Terezín, used professional actors and had therefore a fine professional *niveau*. Unfortunately, the performances settled down to a routine drawing from well tested clichés rather than from the present situation. And this was exactly the opposite of the Czech cabarets. Although most

Terezín "Cafe". Drawing by Bedřich Fritta.

of the actors were amateurs, they substituted enthusiasm for their lack of theatrical experience, especially when directed by politically motivated professionals who addressed themselves to the problems of everyday life.

In December 1942 the *Freizeitgestaltung* was able to open a "café" in Terezín. It did not necessarily mean that the Jews could go there for a little dessert and coffee with a few puffs of a cigarette. From the original drawing it can be seen that all of these things were conspicuously missing. The only thing the afternoon visitors were treated to was being ushered by a "waiter" to a table, where they could sit for the next two hours and listen to music of various instrumental ensembles, some of them especially formed for that purpose. The admission was by ticket, obtainable once in a blue moon from the administration. The ghetto administration acquired some of the previously confiscated instruments stored in Prague, including a grand piano, and daily programs of semiclassical and popular music reminded the visitors better days. Musicians such as Carlo Taube, Kurt Maier, Otto Sattler, and others who had café and nightclub experience, performed with artists who were more at home on a concert stage. Among them was Egon Ledeč, whose *Father's Melody*, written before the war, became a special favorite of the audiences. Carlo Taube formed an orchestra for semiclassical repertoire, while several other groups catered to the jazz-loving public.

The clarinetist, saxophonist, and arranger, Fritz (Bedřich) Weiss,[45] was perhaps the most outstanding jazz player in prewar Czechoslovakia. In Prague he formed a group bearing his own name, the "Jazz-Quintet-Weiss." In the years 1940–41, they used to meet and play in the Jewish orphanage in Prague, and following their arrest they were reunited in Terezín. After some changes in personnel— so frequent in the ghetto—the ensemble achieved the highest artistic calibre with these members: Weiss as clarinetist and leader; Wolfi Lederer, pianist—these two excelling by far the very good reminder of the group; Pavel Libenský played the double bass; Koko Schumann, originally a guitar player, switched successfully to

[45]Also called by the Czech form Fricek.

Fritz (Fricek) Weiss. Drawing by Petr Kien.

percussion; and Franta Goldschmidt was the guitarist, who unfortunately had to play on a very inferior instrument.

Shortly after the establishment of the "café," on January 8, 1943. an engineer and amateur trumpet player, Erich Vogel, sent the following letter to the central administration of the Terezín ghetto:

Theresienstadt, January 8, 1943
To the Central Administration
Att.: Freizeitgestaltung
   This is to inform you that I am planning to make public appearance with a jazz orchestra, which will devote itself chiefly to Jewish music.
The personnel would be:
Piano: Dr. Brammer
Percussion: Dr. Kurt Bauer
Guitar: Fr. Goldschmidt
Bass: Fasal
Trumpet: Ing. Vogel
Tenor Sax and Clarinet: Langer
Trombone: Fr. Mautner
The orchestra would appear under the title:
                THE GHETTO SWINGERS
   I would be greatly obliged if your official in charge of music would get in touch with me in order to be informed thoroughly about our intentions and requests.

                                    Sincerely,
                                    Ing. Erich Vogel.[46]

   The permission was granted, and "The Ghetto Swingers" embarked on their illustrious, though shortlived, career. They joined the ranks of the "café" performers, and their concerts invariably attracted a full house. Obviously, the group was not spared the inevitable changes of personnel, and some of its members belonged also to the Jazz-Quintet-Weiss. The size of the ensemble changed with the musicians and eventually increased in number. When, in 1944, Martin Roman arrived in Terezín, Pavel Libenský, who at that time played the double bass with the Ghetto Swingers, approached him with the

[46]Document from the collection of Dr. H. G. Adler.

151

request that Roman take over the leadership of the orchestra. At first, Roman was reluctant to be in charge of a basically Czech group, but upon Libenský's further insistence, he accepted. Under Roman's baton, the orchestra included three violins, two saxophones, three trumpets, trombone, guitar, accordion, bass, and drums. Roman himself wrote his original compositions and arrangements, conducted, and occasionally played a solo on the piano. As a special attraction, he added a trio of girls singing in the style of the Andrews Sisters, and a tenor, Fredy Haber. Roman's most successful arrangement from his Terezín period was Boulanger's famous tango, "*Avant de mourir*," in which the trio of vocalists alternated with three violins and violin solo, played by Jetti Kantor.[47]

[47]Roman used a renewed version of this arrangement for a recording made several years later in America.

Still from the fraudulent film *Der Führer schenkt de Juden eine Stadt* showing The Ghetto Swingers with their conductor, Martin Roman.

Martin Roman. Photo by Joža Karas.

In the summer of 1944, great changes occurred in Terezín. The town went through a face-lift, *Verschönerung*, as the Germans called it (beautification), and the daily routine of the people improved as well. However, it was not a change of the Nazi heart in their dealings with the Jews. On the contrary, it was one of the most insidious schemes the Nazis could conceive.

To offset the ever increasing worldwide rumors about the bestiality inflicted on the Jewish population in Germany and the German occupied territories, the Nazis decided to produce a "documentary" film about the comfortable life of the Jews under their protection. And what could be a more appropriate setting than the "Terezín Spa?"

153

Once before, some two years earlier, a similar attempt had been made, but the result was so amateurish and "phony" that it could not be shown to even the most naive public. This time the Nazis were more cautious, and every step, every move was made with the utmost care. The movie was produced in connection with the visit of an International Red Cross Committee on June 22, 1944, and, according to Martin Roman, at the direct order of the Propaganda Minister, Josef Goebbels. For that occasion the streets were thoroughly cleaned, literally scrubbed with water and brushes, and houses received a new coat of paint outside and inside, curtains appeared in the windows, the third bunks were taken down, and the problem of overcrowding was "solved" by sending 7,500 old and sick people to the gas chambers in Auschwitz. In the park on the town square, a wooden pavilion had been erected for concerts of Ančerl's string orchestra and Roman's Ghetto Swingers.

Commandant Rahm put Gerron in charge of the whole production, together with the talented painter from the Netherlands, Joe Spier, and the stage director was František Zelenka. Gerron subsequently chose additional coworkers, such as Hans Hofer as his assistant, or Martin Roman, who became responsible for the music. The cameramen, employees of the Czech newsreel *Actualita*, were sent in from Prague, and the cast numbered close to thirty thousand, mostly unwilling actors.

Under the delusive title, *Der Führer schenkt den Juden eine Stadt*, (The Führer donates a town to the Jews), Gerron's carefully prepared scenario showed the "happy life" of the Terezín—and implicitly all other—Jews at the time, when the brave German soldiers were laying down their lives for the *Vaterland*. Various scenes depicted the neat little town from which smiling girls went to work in the nearby fields with a song on their lips; a speech by the Elder Murmelstein; people meeting on the way to do their errands in the shops and a newly erected bank, which was even supplied with specially printed but worthless "ghetto money"; children playing in the playground; sport activities, such as soccer game or swimming; leisurely relaxation in the "café," etc.

Music played an important role in the movie, be it the cheerful singing of the working girls or formal musical performances. Scenes from Krása's children's opera *Brundibár* took turns with people dancing to the tunes of the Ghetto Swingers. As a matter of fact, Roman had to make special "American" arrangements for this occasion. In the pavilion, Karel Ančerl conducted the string orchestra in a performance of a work written for this ensemble by Pavel Haas, the *Study for Strings*. The musicians were issued dark suits with the Star of David on their breasts, of course, but the situation with shoes was somewhat more difficult. The problem was solved ingeniously by placing flower pots along the edge of the podium. Nothing had been omitted. At the conclusion of the composition, the audience applauded enthusiastically when the orchestra with the conductor took their bows and the composer stepped up to acknowledge the success.

The entire production proceeded without a hitch. The Nazis had every reason to be satisfied with the results. They rewarded the main personnel with words of thanks and praise and even some delicacies, stolen from the packages sent to the prisoners by their relatives in the Protectorate. And, above all, they permitted 18,500 "actors" and producers to leave Terezín in the cattle cars heading for Auschwitz. Before boarding one of them, Kurt Gerron heard Rahm's cheery "See you soon!"

Although some of the Terezín inhabitants participated in the production of the film with great enthusiasm, the majority did not want to have anything to do with the deceitful story of this modern day "Potemkin Village."[48] The same applied to the men in charge. Apparently, Kurt Gerron showed reluctance and was coerced into accepting the responsibility through various threats. But what did he gain? Two or three extra months of his life? Or was it the desire of the people to obtain a little special treat, an occasional cigarette, some excitement from the otherwise forbidden games and other activities, or a welcome change from the dreary daily routine that made them submissive to the Nazi whims?

Kurt Gerron never saw the fruits of his labor. The film was developed in Prague, and a copy was sent to Berlin. It was partially

[48]Term referring to the make-believe villages erected for the purpose of impressing the Russian empress Catherine the Great by her advisor, Grigory Aleksandrovich Potemkin.

edited and in March 1945 synchronized with music, but it was never completed. The great hoax of the German Propaganda Ministry found its way only to a few storage closets in Prague and in Israel.

FIFTEEN

Terezín Family Camp in Auschwitz

The history of the musical life in Terezín would not be complete without rendering an account of a bizarre happening miles away, in Auschwitz.

On September, 6, 1943, a transport containing 5007 people left Terezín, heading toward Auschwitz. It was the largest group ever to depart from there in a single day. Although the Nazis called it *Arbeitseinsatztransport* (labor engagement transport), it consisted of entire families, including 285 children under 14 years of age. A Jewish Elder, Dr. Leo Janowitz, one of the closest associates of Jakob Edelstein, was put involuntarily in charge, while the young educator Fredy (Alfred) Hirsch had to accompany the youngsters. And indeed, when the transport arrived in Auschwitz on the next day, its members did not go to an immediate selection. Instead, they were housed in Birkenau, which was the extermination camp in the Auschwitz complex. Surprisingly enough, they could keep their belongings, did not get the regular "total" haircut, and even kept their civilian clothes rather than exchanging them for prisoners' uniforms. This then was the beginning of the existence of the so-called *Theresienstadt Familienlager* (Terezín Family Camp) in Auschwitz-Birkenau.

The daily routine in this camp was very different from the one in Terezín. Families were again separated, but they could visit frequently, since people did not have to work. To top it off, they even received white bread. Actually, the busiest members of the transport were the children. In their special block, they had to attend school, directed by Fredy Hirsch, complete with a library, which was something unheard of in Auschwitz, where books were strictly forbidden. Particular consideration was given once more to musical education, mainly singing. Children participated in several choirs and also had the opportunity to attend recitals of chamber music.

One of the highlights in the musical life of the camp was the presentation of a "children's opera" based on the story of Snow White and called in German *Schneewittchen*. It hardly deserved the title of opera, since it was not an original composition but rather a simple children's play, supplemented by melodies of Czech folksongs with new German lyrics, some of them especially written for the occasion of Hirsch's birthday. Due to the unavailability of a piano accompaniment, a mouth harmonica had to suffice.

Similarly, the repertoire of the choral groups comprised mainly folksongs, although here and there more sophisticated music had been used. It had to be shocking to hear the melody from Beethoven's Ninth Symphony, to the words of *Ode to Joy* by Friedrich Schiller, as it almost reached the crematoria from the nearby children's block. Maybe it was a good thing that the children did not comprehend the meaning of what they were singing. Otto Dov Kulka, one of the young participants, has the following fond recollection:

> Here I have to remark that long time later, several months after the complete liquidation of the camp, I found a harmonica and I played on it the tune from this Ode. And that time, a young prisoner, I believe he was from Berlin, a Jew, asked me if I knew what I was actually playing. I told him it was a piece that we had sung in the so-called family camp. Then he mentioned the name of the symphony, the name of Ludwig van Beethoven, told me about Beethoven, about Schiller, and

explained to me the meaning of the text. Since that time, I hold this in my remembrances as one of the most curious experiences of this stay, one which I started to understand already then, after the liquidation of the camp.[49]

The musical performances had been attended by the other prisoners from the family camp as well as the SS and their henchmen, the Kapos. The same SS who applauded the *Ode to Joy* led the same children to their doom in Birkenau's crematoria a few weeks later. Because that is exactly what they had in store for them from the moment of their arrival in Auschwitz.

Even more surprising are the testimonies of a few survivors, according to which these Jewish children sang Nazi songs. A Polish Kapo, Bednarik, had a good rapport with the children, and they would often gather around him and listen as he sang the only tunes he knew—the Nazi songs—usually without words. The children in their innocence and naiveté would join him: *"Leb' wohl, mein Schatz, lebe wohl! Denn wir fahren gegen Engeland. . . . "* (Goodbye, my darling, goodbye! For we are going against England).

Back in Terezín, rumors started spreading that the so-called "labor transport" was nothing but a cover name for a departure to annihilation. The Jewish Elder, Jakob Edelstein, therefore visited the camp commander, Seidl, and asked him directly if there was any truth to these rumors. He received assurances that they were exactly that—rumors. However, was it just a coincidence that, not much later, on November 9, 1943, Edelstein was arrested and put into one of the two transports that left again for the Terezín family camp in Birkenau, on December 15 or 18? His deputy, Otto Zucker, replaced him at the helm of the Council of Elders.

Similar anxieties settled upon the people in the family camp itself. Rumors persisted that the present arrangement was only temporary, and that all of the inmates would eventually end in the gas chambers. In that event there was nothing to lose, and so several members of the first transport, Fredy Hirsch among them, started to

---

[49]From the testimony of Otto Dov Kulka: *Bericht über das "Theresienstädter Familienlager" in Auschwitz-Birkenau.*

organize a resistance group which would start an open revolt in case of executions. The much feared day finally arrived on March 7, 1944, exactly half a year after the arrival of the transport at Auschwitz. It also happened to be the birthday of Tomáš G. Masaryk, the first president of Czechoslovakia. The Nazis liked to execute their victims on memorable days, such as religious holidays and other days of significance. Fredy Hirsch saw the inevitable coming, but he also realized that people would not start an uprising, and, in desperation, he took poison on the preceding night. He did not die instantly, and the next day he was carried unconscious into the gas chamber. Of the total of more than five thousand people from that fateful transport, only thirty-seven boys survived. The others awaited the turning on of the deadly Zyklon-B with the Czech national anthem and the Hatikva on their lips.

Finally, three more transports arrived from Terezín in May 1944, totaling more than 7,500 people. Then in July they went, together with the members of the December transport, for selection. This time about 1,200 were spared and sent away to labor camps, and the senseless history of the Terezín family camp ended with the annihilation of all the others on July 14, 1944.

What was the purpose of this so-called "Family camp," and why had the Nazis delayed the executions?

From the existing documents and testimonies it becomes obvious that the Terezín family camp in Birkenau served the same purpose as the original Terezín in Bohemia—a "Potemkin village." Immediately after their arrival, people had to write letters to their relatives and friends in Terezín and elsewhere and tell them about their new and improved living conditions. This went on until March 5, 1944, when the people from the first transport were ordered to write postcards dated some three weeks later. On that same day, they were also separated from the December transport with the understanding that they would go to a new family camp, *"Familienlager Heydebreck."* At the time of their "departure" their fears were momentarily appeased. They had been loaded into trucks and taken away in the direction out of the camp. But not for long. After a small detour, the trucks stopped not far from the point of departure and unloaded the "cargo" right into the gas chambers. The December arrivals observed the supposed situation with satisfaction, and subsequently reported the "good news," supported by the predated postcards back to Terezín.

A second explanation for the rather strange arrangements and fate of the people in the "Terezín family camp" suggests that the Nazis planned a visit of the German Red Cross delegation to Auschwitz, similar to the one which took place in June 1943 in Terezín. The "Terezín" in Birkenau had been considered for this honor; however, the visit never materialized.

The exemption from the execution for the thirty-seven boys from the first transport was very possibly also a part of the whole camouflage scheme, supposedly proving that the Nazis did not execute children. The larger number of able-bodied survivors from the following transports indicated only the ever increasing need for a labor force in the sagging Third Reich. The Jews had to work for the victory of their tormentors, and when their bodies were completely drained of the last drop of energy, there was always time enough for their extermination.

SIXTEEN

Journey to the East

On October 16, 1944, the musical life in Terezín was left in shambles. This in itself would not have been a tragedy; on the contrary, it could have been the most joyful occasion if the prisoners were permitted to return home. But it became a real tragedy, a small part of the enormous overall Jewish tragedy.

More than half a year before the end of the war in Europe, it was obvious that the German empire, built by Hitler to last for the next thousand years, was suffering the last contractions of a dying beast. The Allied armies were pressing hard from all sides, and the German-occupied territories were shrinking every day. The Russian army made rapid advances as the German High Command "pulled back their troops for tactical reasons in order to shorten the front,"[50] and was approaching the "death factory" in Auschwitz-Birkenau. Hitler's fury reached the climax, and the gas chambers and ovens of the crematoria in the extermination camps were swallowing their victims twenty-four hours daily like an insatiable seven-headed dragon.

---

[50]Phrase used by the Nazis in reports from the Russian front, camouflaging the admission of a defeat or retreat.

It was—so to speak—the last chance to liquidate the Terezín prisoners. Therefore, in one month, between September 28 and October 28, 1944, 11 transports relocated 18,500 people from Terezín to Auschwitz, in addition to the 5,000 who had proceeded them in the transport on September 23. The transport on October 16 had the rare distinction that this time a great number of musicians were included. Until then, the artists enjoyed some protection through the efforts of Dr. Otto Zucker, who now became one of the departees. This prompted several musicians to volunteer for the trip to the East in the false hope that he would be able to shield them once again in another concentration camp. The Ghetto Swingers, side by side with almost the entire string orchestra of Karel Ančerl, which only a few days earlier performed the premiere of Pavel Haas' *Study for Strings*, were on board the train. Together with them were the composers and other musicians who had taken part in the rich musical life of the Terezín ghetto, such as Viktor Ullmann, Hans Krása, Rafael Schächter, Egon Ledeč, Bernard Kaff, and Karel Ančerl, just to mention a few of the best known. With the exception of the last one, all the aforementioned were executed immediately after their arrival, including Dr. Zucker.

On October 17 the train came to a stop at its destination, Auschwitz. The much-feared Dr. Josef Mengele personally supervised the selection on the platform. Alas, damned were all those who happened to wear glasses or who had red hair! In danger also were men past forty years of age. Upon seeing them, Mengele pointed his ominous finger to the right, from where there was no return.[51] The majority of the newly arrived went from the station platform directly into the gas chambers stark naked, after all their belongings had been confiscated.

Mengele had the habit of asking people about their profession, which sometimes influenced his decision. Karel Berman, who came to Auschwitz a few days earlier, recalled the tragic story of his friend and colleague František Weissenstein. Truthfully answering Mengele's question, Weissenstein gave his occupation as singer—and was sent to the right. Berman, who followed him, on a spur of the moment

---

[51]Some witnesses quote "right" as being assigned to work, and "left" as condemnation.

declared that he was a worker, and that saved his life. Another heartbreaking incident, as related by Karel Ančerl, concerned the pianist Bernard Kaff. A little man with very poor eyesight, Kaff was standing behind Ančerl, who was in Terezín employed as a cook and therefore was a little better fed and heavier. Ančerl tried to shield his friend with his body, but Kaff stuck out his head from behind him in order to see what was happening, and for that one glance he paid with his life. Mengele noticed the head with the very thick glasses whose wearer could not possibly be of much help to the final victory of the Third Reich, and Bernard Kaff was ordered to join the long line heading for the gas chambers. And of course, the clarinetist Friedrich Weiss did not have any chance with his "winning" combination of glasses *and* red hair!

Several able-bodied younger men survived the ordeal, and after a short stay in Auschwitz they continued on their way to work in other concentration camps. In his memoirs, Karel Berman described his dreadful odyssey with the following expressive words:

> Suddenly, a transport is called—"for work in Dresden"—all young able-bodied men, up to fifty years of age (later to sixty-five). And on September 28, 1944, we departed. Ústí nad Labem—Dresden. We send postcards to Terezín, announcing safe arrival, and two hours later we are going again—destination unknown. Two days later, about one o'clock at night, we stop. Our blood gets chilly when we see through a little window of a sealed boxcar (there are sixty-five of us) the station sign: AUSCHWITZ. Forcefully we are separated from our luggage. Lined up in double column we march past the SS. One of them (the infamous Dr. Mengele) points out where we should go—right, left. We are putting our fate in God's hands, and when the SS points to the left, we go there. In front of us we can see only wires, concrete pillars, shooting ranges, machine-gun nests, and SS men with rifles. There in the back some building with a tall chimney, from which flames flare unceasingly ten to twenty meters high. We have no idea what it is, what is being readied for us, nothing, nothing. (The next day we find out that friends who went from the train to the right are no longer alive, that they went into the gas chambers, and there in that building with the chimney, spitting flames, they were burned.) Terror which is

being readied for us, we realize, when we live it through. On the whole: In the first room give away money, fountain pen, gold, etc., in the second take off all clothing except shoes, belt, and spectacles. In the third we are standing naked pressed to each other (eternity), in the fourth we are completely scraped with dull blades (all over the body, wherever there is a single hair), bleeding we march into the fifth room—under showers, hot-cold, then, as we are passing in line, they smear us with Lysol liquid and throw us a shirt, something like underwear (it is from Tallin), pants, socks, coat, and then throw us still wet into October frost. They lead us into the barracks, squeeze about twelve of us on each cot, and let us, this way, "rest."

And then, during the day, we stand outside in all kinds of weather and at night we are squeezed inside, until one day an order comes that those who reported as workers (I was one of them) will pass one more selection by Mengele, and according to his decision, they either will go to work in Germany or into gas chambers.

Some six to eight days later (I do not know how long we stayed there) again the procedure of washing, smearing with Lysol, and changing of clothes, and we are led in the midst of machine-guns to the boxcars. They press about seventy to seventy-five of us into each one, give us a loaf of bread, a piece of salami, and margarine, seal the box cars, and we sigh with relief when the train starts moving, be it anyplace, as long as it is away from this horrible sight of the flames from the crematorium, which stopped working, during our entire sojourn there, for only about half an hour. And again, we are going to an unknown destination, tears in our eyes when we stop in Olomouc and hear Czech spoken in front of the boxcars. Later we pass Vienna, Salzburg, and after three nights and two days we disembark at the railroad station Kauffering by Landsberg on Lech. The SS hands us over to the *Wehrmacht* (army), and that kindles in us a little spark of hope for better treatment.

From the railroad station we marched a long time on the road through woods and ditches. It must be a beautiful sight: two thousand fatigued men in a cordon of raised rifles. Late at night we arrived—to barbed wires. Concentration camp Kauffering II. Lined up and accounted for, we received blankets, and then they chased us like a herd into some underground barracks. One could not see anything, but the reception was nice—a blow on the head with a club. Only in the morning we saw where we were. A few wooden barracks for the "VIPs" (*Kapos*—watchmen). For the *häftlings* (captives) barracks— holes in the ground with wooden planks covered with straw for sleeping. Above the ground, only a small roof covered with dirt and overgrown grass. In each barrack sixty to seventy people. After several days of counting and registering we are assigned to different *commandos* (details) for better or worse work.

For a long period of time, I was a member of a group which was building some huge underground factory, probably for airplanes; that was the "Holzmann *commando*." Each morning waking up at 4:30, ration of black coffee and bread (at the beginning a little more, later the rations got damned smaller), and at about 5:00 a.m. we had to stand outside in the courtyard. Divided into *commandos* (that took sometimes up to two hours—but I experienced some roll-calls during the winter in snow and mud which lasted four to five hours) and we go to work. At noon half an hour for swallowing the soup (it was actually plain warm water, but upon closer examination one could find a little shred of cabbage). And again work, mixing concrete, carrying rails or heavy tree trunks, move boulders and level the ground, and again maybe the rails or trunks and boulders move back to the original place. One friend, overfatigued from the work at night, goes unnoticed to take a rest behind a tool shed, but the SS man sees everything, and the next moment the poor wretch has two bullets in his head.

For a short time I joined the shirkers in the *commando* of ten people who were catering to the SS men. It had the advantage that one could eat a little more. Alarm worse than air attack alarms: a typhoid epidemic broke out. People fell of exhaustion like flies; dysentery and typhoid finished without mercy those with weak will to overcome it. I resisted for a long time, working as a barber in the sick-bay, but in vain. They carried me into the quarantine block and threw me on a board. I could not move any longer, having a temperature of 41 centigrade, so they stole everything I still owned, clothes which I received for my singing, shoes which I was able to keep even in Auschwitz, even the cup and spoon, and so I was lying naked, helpless, full of lice under and above the blanket, for ten days, unconscious, only dreaming all the time about the gate of heaven, in front of which I was sitting and asking for entrance so that I could sing in heaven. After ten days the fever suddenly disappeared and I was alive, to the surprise of the caretaking doctors and those who felt sympathy toward me, and even to my own surprise. However, I could not get up on my feet, and since I had to be transferred to the convalescence block, where only a few lucky ones went, I received an order: "Come quickly!" However, when I did not have enough strength to even sit up, two male nurses took me between them, pulled me by the hands on the ground in the mud, and dumped me in the "delousing station" under hot water; several of such Lazaruses were there, one colleague expired immediately upon the contact with water. Then I crawled, I do not recall how, into another room where I obtained a coat and pants and, thanks to acquaintances from the sick-bay, I was thrown over the shoulder like a bag of flour and carried to the convalescent block. There a friend was already expecting me, the only Czech-feeling physician (contrary to all others, including male nurses, Hungarians, loathsome and pitiless creatures with human appearance). Immediately they gave me soup and another one and still another. . . . I ate like crazy until I got diarrhea that I thought I would not survive. And I lost so much weight that my thigh was about as thick as my forearm now. And instead of my buttocks only rags of wrinkled skin; at that time I weighed, according to my estimate, about thirty-eight to forty kilos, if that much. And I overcame even the diarrhea, and then, after some fourteen days, I started to learn walking, like a baby—two steps, flop, they had to pick me up, and again new tries and then I crossed the whole block, once, twice, three times, and it did not take long, and I had to march twelve kilometers nonstop, we were moving to Kauffering IV.

The first person I met there was a friend from Terezín, who began taking care of me immediately; with three other colleagues we formed a "Cabaret commando," and we did nothing but rehearse for the cabaret and performed the show for the *lager* commandant. We had good soup three times a day (instead of once) and then we received daily a bag of potato peels and scrapings which served us remarkably for making various dishes which will probably never be surpassed taste-wise.

The end of the war is approaching; we have the battlefield right behind the camp, and we are looking forward to an early liberation when an order comes: the healthy line up, the sick remain, the camp is being evacuated. And so I decided, no matter how weak I was, to go and eventually perish of exhaustion on the road, rather than stay behind and be shot as an invalid. And again the will power and the desire for survival and meeting with the loved ones triumphed. I marched seventy-nine kilometers to Allach by Dachau, and although I was exhausted to death, I survived that terror. There the *Hitlerjugend* shot into us with anti-aircraft guns, and a number of people, the healthy ones, paid for it, but the next day in festive anticipation (when we realized that the SS men had disappeared) we were liberated by the American army."[52]

[52]Used with permission of the author.

Karel Berman, member of the National Theater in Prague.

SEVENTEEN

Meanwhile in Terezín. . .

The departure of a great number of musicians from Terezín in the fall of 1944 certainly shocked the entire artistic community. There are no available weekly programs of the *Freizeitgestaltung* which would show the exent of limitation of musical performances. Understandably, all operatic productions were out of the question, together with performances of ensembles, whether Ančerl's string orchestra or various chamber groups. Artists left behind were mostly women, such as the pianists Alice Herz Sommer and Edith Steiner-Kraus, singers Marion Polodier, Hedda Grab-Kernmayr, Ada Schwarz-Klein, Hilde Aronson-Lindt, and a few others. The Danish conductor Peter Deutsch also remained in Terezín, because the Danish prisoners, protected by their king, could not be sent to extermination camps. As a matter of fact, shortly before the liberation, on April 15, 1945, all of them were released into the custody of the Swedish Red Cross and taken to Sweden. Only after the war could they return to their homeland.

A great advantage was bestowed upon the Jews from mixed marriages. For the most part they stayed at home, and only as late as the autumn of 1944 and at the beginning of 1945 had they been rounded up and imprisoned in concentration camps. Thus new artistic blood was injected into the sagging musical life in Terezín.

171

From Prague came the conductor Robert Brock, the excellent basso and stage director from the National Theater, Hanuš Thein, and the violinist Paul Herz, brother of Alice Herz Sommer. Another first-rate violinist arrived from the Netherlands, Prof. Hermann Leydensdorff, and a number of other artists and amateurs started to appear on the musical programs once more.

As the officers of the *Freizeitgestaltung* left for Auschwitz, apparently it took a while before this group was reorganized. However, the musical activities rose once again to unusual standards. Alice Herz Sommer presented an all-Chopin recital on Febraury 7, 1945. The unsigned review from the pen of a writer waiting for an early return home to Munich is worth citing in its entirety:

> The art-loving Theresienstadt stood last night, February 7, 1945, under the sign of a great Chopin-evening by Mrs. Herz Sommer. I have heard Raoul Koschalski, student of (Anton) Rubinstein, whose Master was Chopin himself, and still I dare to make a comparison. When France calls her great tragedienne, Sarah Bernhardt, the "Divine Sarah," why shouldn't we call the great interpreter of Chopin, Mrs. Herz Sommer, Chopin's "Divine Mirror." Obviously, one speaks of heavy and delicate ways of playing Chopin's works; however, these two types so interwined in one person have never reached my inner ear in the manner of the powerful interpretation by Mrs. Herz Sommer. Since I, as a critic, will hand over these lines in the nearest possible future to a Munich musical periodical, and, above all, because I must take into consideration the lack of space today, I have to and will disregard the analytic definition and criticism of individual pieces, and in my discussion I will restrict myself solely to the performance of the works brought to hearing by Mrs. Herz Sommer.
>
> The unusually large format of her playing, which grabs powerfully the soul of the listener, lies, first of all, in the diction of her musical language, which rouses every soul and thrusts upon it her own individual understanding. Her wonderful playing pulls out the registers of melancholy, passion, and powerful happening like the captivating charm of the French temperament, precisely those qualities which are embodied most significantly in the ailing nature of the composer.

When the artist unleashes with magic vibrations of her fingers real storms of her mind, in which the peculiar mixture of the character of two nations, the Slavic and the French, steps before the spiritual eye, then the genius of the Muse stood certainly by her as a godparent, and the listening audience kneels before her tonal interpretation as in prayer. This rare artist does not only master sovereignly the musical idea, but with all the voluminous power of Chopin's works she is an engraver of the most daintily carved ornamentation and the most exquisite sound-stylization. Her playing consists of a prologue, followed by a classic dialogue in pearl-like catharsis, only to submerge into melancholic elegy, to rise up in rapid strides, to proclaim in majestic ecstasy the hymns of the most noble art. "Be embraced, all ye millions," you who live for art and her Muse. And when, on behalf of all mankind, I lament here and deplore the early and young life of a Master prematurely snatched away from the world, and when I allow the divine inspiration of this immortal Master to sound inside my own self, I arrive ever more distinctly and with deeper seriousness at the conviction: This inspiration, full of melancholy and sweetness of the young Chopin, only one interpreter can make immortal in innate perfection, through the reincarnation and resurrection, and this is— by the grace of God—the artist: Mrs. Herz Sommer."[53]

The pianist repeated the successful program several times until April 14, 1945, and five days later she presented still another recital of works by Schubert and Schumann. When her brother Paul Herz arrived, they played Beethoven's sonatas for piano and violin, and both of them took part in other musical offerings.

Edith Steiner Kraus kept similarly busy at the piano with ten repetitions of an all-Bach program, consisting of the *Partita in D Major*, three Preludes and Fugues from the *Well-Tempered Clavier*, and the *Chromatic Fantasy and Fugue*. In collaboration with the pianists Beatrice Pimentel and Elsa Schiller, respectively, she participated in evenings of music for two pianos and additional concerts.

---

[53]Unsigned document from the collection of Mrs. Herz Sommer, used with her permission. Translation by the author.

Noteworthy was the entrance of Professor Hermann Leydensdorff on the Terezín musical scene. He became, more or less, the heir to the responsibilities of Karel Fröhlich. Teamed with Elsa Schiller, he introduced and repeated Mozart sonatas for violin and piano, besides participation in various concerts and recitals. Leydensdorff took over the concertmaster's chair in an orchestra led in public performances of light music by Peter Deutsch and in presentation of operatic melodies under the baton of Leo Pappenheim, who came to the ghetto from the Netherlands. This orchestra sprang to life from the ruins of the string orchestra of Karel Ančerl through the revival efforts of Pappenheim and Robert Brock. Thanks to similar efforts of Hans Feith, jazz music found its way back to the Terezín stages in the form of a new jazz quintet under his direction.

Brock's first job in Terezín was as a "horse." This meant that he and several other inmates had to pull the old-fashioned hearse in which bread was carried around the town for distribution and bodies were taken out for burial. Only after some time was he assigned to the *Freizeitgestaltung* as conductor of the orchestra. In this capacity he prepared again the *Serenade for Strings* of Antonín Dvořák and some music by Bohuslav Martinů, but these compositions were never played for the public. However, Brock became involved in one very exciting undertaking.

As the end of the war was approaching, the Nazis were trying to gather more and more alibis. One way of doing so was through the inspections of the camp by the representatives of the Red Cross. They could not impress the visitors with *Brundibár* and Verdi's *Requiem* anymore, because most of the performers had gone with the last transports to Auschwitz. But the children's presentations were always very effective; and so one night in March the *lager* commandant called Hanuš Thein and barked at him: *"Ich brauche eine Kinderoper!"* (I need a children's opera!) For Thein this was a tremendous opportunity to work in his profession, but he realized the impossibility of the request. Humperdinck's *Hänsel und Gretel* was too difficult, and nothing else was on hand. In the ensuing sleepless night, Thein suddenly remembered rumors which had been circulating in Prague about the Terezín production of a famous Czech fairytale,

Broučci (Fireflies). In the morning he looked up Vlasta Schönová, who was responsible for previous presentations, and Robert Brock, and asked them for their assistance.

The story of the *Fireflies* and its significance in Terezín deserves a more in-depth explanation. The book had been written by a Czech Protestant minister, Jan Karafiát, at the beginning of this century, and immediately it became a classic in children's literature. Through adventures of a little firefly boy, it instills the highest moral principles into children's minds.

Back in 1943 in Terezín, the governess Kamila Rosenbaum used to read the book to her wards. Being a professional dancer, formerly employed in the avant-garde Theater D-34 in Prague, she taught the children to express the story through dance. Then one day she asked Vlasta Schönová to collaborate with her on a presentation in which the children would dance while Schönová read the story. The young aspiring actress liked the idea very much, and she readily accepted the invitation with the provision that she could change the concept. Subsequently, Schönová dramatized the book and the children had to act as well as dance, while she recited only the text connecting various scenes. In this form the play was performed about twenty-eight times, until the extermination transports in October 1944. According to the written memoirs of Vlasta Schönová, her dramatization of *Fireflies* included Czech folksongs arranged by Karel Švenk. On the other hand, in a taped interview with the author of this book, she specified that these performances were without any musical background.

The resurgence of *Fireflies* occurred in March 1945. At first, Schönová declined Thein's invitation to take part in any production for the Germans and their efforts to falsify the living conditions in Terezín. Thein, on the other hand, claimed great patriotic significance for the endeavor. After a long argument he convinced her, and she proceeded with the preparations in conformity with the previous production as conceived by Kamila Rosenbaum, who in the meantime had been sent to Auschwitz. Robert Brock received an order from the Nazis to compose music in three days. After a consultation with Thein and Schönová, they decided on the use of Czech folksongs.

To enable Brock to meet the deadline, the SS gave him an extra room for working and even brought him coffee during the night so that he would not fall asleep.

The premiere of the new version took place on the stage of the "Sokolovna" hall on March 20, 1945. The representatives of the Red Cross attended one of the performances, but it is doubtful that it was the first one. The audience was treated to more than the Nazis were hoping for. The conductor raised the baton, and the orchestra of some thirty musicians, many of them Danish, began the overture, which was actually not more than a medley of songs. An acute ear could, however, soon recognize the tune of the Czech national anthem, cleverly concealed in the contrapuntal middle voices—a rather audacious deed on the part of the composer. Then the curtain rose and unveiled the brightly lit stage, full of enormous flowers, among which the children looked really like little fireflies. They acted, danced, sang, and between the scenes Vlasta Schönová, sitting in the pit right beside the conductor, read the connecting lines. Not being too musically inclined, she had to be prompted once in a while by Brock's fatherly nudge, but otherwise everything went very smoothly, to the public's delight. Thein with his beautiful basso sang several times *U panského dvora* (At the Lord's courtyard) and some other folksongs. When the children plunged into the song *Přijde jaro, přijde, zase bude máj* (Spring will come soon, May will be here again), only a few eyes in the audience remained dry, because the song represented for the people the coming end of their horrible oppression. How right they were! On May 5 the SS fled from Terezín, and three days later the concentration camp was liberated. And so, what was supposed to be a little entertainment for the visitors and a lot of Nazi propaganda turned into a major manifestation of patriotism. It is significant that the play was performed in the Czech language at a time when only German utterances were permitted by the authorities. Still, the Nazis were satisfied, and Thein received the biggest reward in his career for his contribution —a can of liver paté!

Fireflies ran for about fifteen performances, with the last scheduled in the second half of April. It did not take place, because that afternoon several trains arrived loaded with people more dead than alive, and the Terezín inhabitants had to come to their aid. Thein himself assisted at a car from which they pulled some twenty corpses. This was not bad enough. Several of the newcomers were afflicted with typhus and had to be isolated, with very strict hygienic measures taken.

The final major musical offering in Terezín happened, like *Fireflies*, on the direct order of the *lager* commander. Once again he summoned Hanuš Thein to his office and asked him to stage a performance of *The Tales of Hoffmann* by Jacques Offenbach. To Thein's astonishment, he accompanied his request by throwing at his feet the complete score of the opera from the archives of the National Theater in Prague. As Thein found out after the war, an austere order came to the theater from the Gestapo to "deliver immediately the score of *The Tales of Hoffmann* of the Jew Offenbach to Terezín." Thein accepted the dictate quite enthusiastically, since it offered him the chance to work again in his field and, above all, he could present a piece by a Jewish composer, something that could not have been done during all the war years. One unpleasant condition was attached: the opera had to be shortened to about an hour. But how does one preserve a masterpiece if one has to eliminate more than half of it?

Since Necessity is the Mother of Invention, Thein found a way to cope with the double task successfully. He kept the entire Prologue and Epilogue of the opera, and in between he used the famous aria from the first act, the indispensable Barcarolle from the second, and the whole third act. The soloists' ensemble of extraordinary quality was headed by an excellent Slovak tenor, Dr. Blum, in the role of Hoffmann, and the opera was expertly conducted by Leo Pappenheim. The presentation resulted also in a lecture, "The Meaning of *The Tales of Hoffmann*," given by Hans Epstein on April 17, a week after the premiere.

As a postscript to the production of the opera, Thein found the score during his departure from Terezín someplace in the "Sokolovna" hall. He wrapped it up and put in a safe place and after his return to the National Theater he instructed the librarian as to its whereabouts. The latter then found everything exactly as he had been told. Thein himself would not go back to Terezín.

EIGHTEEN

... And Those Who Survived

The war drew relentlessly to an end, expected in anxious anticipation by the thousands of prisoners in the concentration camps as well as millions of weary people on both sides. Finally, the last concentration camp had been liberated, but this did not mean that the inmates could necessarily go home right away. Epidemics, illnesses, and general weakness caused postponement of repatriation until health conditions improved to such an extent that the journey home did not jeopardize the well-being of all involved.

The last days in Terezín were chaotic. In the middle of April, the Danish Jews were sent to Sweden through the efforts of the Swedish Red Cross. Several transports arrived from other concentration camps and with them a number of former Terezín prisoners; and so the population rose to more than 17,500 inhabitants. Then, on April 24, a new complication appeared: typhus epidemic. In the meantime, the representatives of the International Red Cross were negotiating with the Nazis, and as a result they took charge of the camp on May 2. By May 5 the number of inmates had swollen to 30,000. Also, on that day they saw for the last time the hated SS men as they pulled out of Terezín in defeat. On May 8 the revolution in Prague ended with the German capitulation, and at nine o'clock in the evening Terezín was liberated. Finally, on May 10, the Red Army entered the town and assumed responsibilities from the hands of the Red Cross.

Because of the typhus epidemic, the freed prisoners could not leave Terezín for another two weeks of strict quarantine, and only after that, depending on the result of a thorough examination, could they begin their journey home. At the end of June there were still almost six thousand people in Terezín, and it was only on August 17, 1945, that the town was ready to welcome back its original inhabitants.

The situation in other concentration camps did not differ much from the one in Terezín. Let us return once more to Karel Berman's memoirs and his eloquent description of the final events:

> They (the American army liberating Kauffering) gave us macaroni with pork and so from the three week quarantine we spent fourteen days in the latrine (and quite a few people even died), but we were free. First greetings to Czechoslovakia, the announcement that we are alive, and finally, on May 23, the big delousing and putting on clean clothes and SS uniforms. The wooden shoes (I wore on my right foot size about 45 and on the left 42—my feet are 41;[54] and in those I underwent the evacuation march) we exchanged for SS felt boots, on the sleeve the tricolor band, early to bed, early to get up, and at six o'clock in the morning we started in the direction Munich, Železná Ruda.
>
> And so, I survived concentration camps, compared to which the terrors of hell are just about like lemonade compared to Lysol. And that only through strong will, powerful will, and the infinite desire to meet my parents and my brother.
>
> On May 24, 1945, at 9:30 a.m. we crossed the border of free Czechoslovakia in the Šumava region. Until six in the afternoon we remained in Plzeň, and on May 25, 1945, we traveled from Plzeň to Prague.

[54]Size number in European measurements (41 is equivalent roughly to size 10).

180

From the whole family on my father's and mother's side, I met only one of my mother's brothers, his wife, and my mother's niece. All the others perished, Lord knows where and how.

I am beginning a new life!"[55]

Yes, indeed, Karel Berman and his surviving colleagues started new lives—in many cases very illustrious ones.

After the war, Berman returned to the Prague Conservatory and graduated in 1946 as a singer and stage director. Following shorter stints in smaller theaters he was engaged by the National Theater in Prague, the foremost operatic scene in Czechoslovakia. His roles spanned Leporello in *Don Giovanni* to Boris Godunov, composers from Pergolesi to Alban Berg; he sang lieder and songs as well as oratorios, and was at home with equal ease on a podium, in a recording studio, or as a stage director in theater or television. He is today in great demand on European operatic stages and has sung also in Japan. In 1971, as a special guest, Berman took part in the first performance of music from Terezín in America, a television program called "There shall be heard again. . . . "

Of all the artists who lived in Terezín, Karel Ančerl became the best known around the whole world. After the occupation he resumed his previous job as conductor on Prague radio. Subsequently he conducted the Grand Opera in Prague, became artistic director of the Radio Symphony Orchestra, and finally, in 1950, he was appointed to the same function at the helm of the famous Czech Philharmonic. With them and as a guest conductor he visited all five continents. In 1969 Ančerl accepted the leadership of the Toronto Symphony, a post he held until his death on July 3, 1973. His numerous phonograph recordings encompass not only works from the standard repertoire but also less known compositions of contemporary Czechoslovak composers.

Upon his return from Terezín, Robert Brock (born 1905) became a conductor in the opera house in Brno in 1945, and two years later he moved to Prague, first as director of the Grand Opera and since 1948 as assistant director of the National Theater. In the same year

---

[55]Used with permission of the author.

he began teaching conducting at the Academy of Musical Arts in Prague. He retired in 1974, and passed away in 1979.

The composer-conductor, Peter Deutsch, was born in Berlin in 1901. There he received his musical education and commenced writing music for films. It was a stroke of luck when he moved to Denmark in 1929 to continue composing for films, theater and radio. He came to Terezín with the Danish Jews and thus avoided an eventual transport to Auschwitz. After the war, Deutsch returned to Copenhagen and resumed his work, writing also smaller pieces for orchestra, as well as light music, often under the pseudonym of Pete Alman. From 1951 to 1955, he conducted the Danish Youth Symphony Orchestra, and thereafter the Copenhagen Municipal School Orchestra. He died in Copenhagen on May 13, 1965.

The Dutch conductor, Leo Pappenheim, born in 1896, had an impressive career behind him, when he came to Terezín. Since the age of twenty, he conducted orchestras and operas in Germany and Holland, finally becoming the head of the Arnhem Orchestral Society, in 1939. After his release from the concentration camp, he returned to his post in Arnhem (the Society changed its name to Gelders Orchestra), where he stayed until 1961. However, he remained very active, conducting various Dutch and German orchestras, notably Radio Hilversum and the Beethoven-Halle Orchestra in Bonn, until his complete retirement in 1975. He died in Arnhem in 1982.

The conductor of *Brundibár*, Rudolf Freudenfeld, survived Auschwitz and came back home to his original vocation as educator. He changed his German name to Franěk, and under this name is known as the director of a secondary school in Prague, the former Academic Gymnasium.

Of the Terezín composers, only two were lucky enough to survive the war, and both of them played only a minor role in the concentration camp. Even in his youth, Karel Reiner had been oriented to avant-garde music, and he appeared as a pianist in countless performances of contemporary music, including compositions written in the quarter-tone system. His compositions followed the examples of his mentor, Alois Hába; but after the war

Reiner directed his creativity to a more conservative expression. He had been since his youth a follower of the Communist movement, and it is therefore not surprising that he turned his attention in the postwar era to composition of socialistic songs with titles such as *The Rocket with a Red Banner, The War Atom, No, Yankee, No,* etc. He is also the author of symphonic music, chamber music, vocal works, and film music. In this category we have to mention the Suite from the movie, *The Butterflies Do Not Live Here,* which is based on the drawings and poetry of the children incarcerated in Terezín.

The other surviving composer, František Domažlický, was born in 1913. In Terezín he was still a musical dilettante. Only after the war did he start to study violin and composition seriously, at the Academy of Musical Arts in Prague. His symphonic compositions can be heard frequently in Europe, and occasionally also on this side of the Atlantic.

Several violinists achieved considerable success upon their release from the concentration camps. Karel Fröhlich studied violin at the Prague Conservatory and the Master School until 1940. Before his departure for Terezín, he concertized under an assumed name, and after his return was engaged as concertmaster in the Grand Opera in Prague. He gave recitals in France, Belgium, and the United States, where he settled in 1948.

The two young budding artists, Pavel (Paul) Kling (born 1928) and Tomáš (Thomas) Mandl (born 1926), embarked on solo and teaching careers once they had finished their interrupted education. After the completion of his violin studies at the Academy of Musical Arts in Prague, Kling spent several years in Japan as concertmaster and leader of a string quartet. Later he moved to the United States and joined the Louisville Symphony Orchestra as concertmaster, while teaching at the University of Louisville, Kentucky. Despite his double duties, he still finds time for a busy solo schedule.

Tomáš Mandl studied violin at the State Conservatory in Brno and graduated from the Academy in Prague in 1954. Since that year he has combined teaching at the conservatory in Ostrava (Czecho-slovakia) with a solo career together with his wife, pianist Jaroslava Mandl. From 1960 on, he concertized in West European countries, and in 1969 he took up residence in Tacoma, Washington, for a few years as violin teacher and recitalist. At the present time he is continuing his musical activities once more in West Germany.

As of this writing, Hermann Leydensdorff (born 1891) was still living in Naarden, Holland. Although he acknowledged the author's letter, he preferred not to comment on his activities before or after the war.

The two most prominent pianists who stayed in Terezín until the liberation did not remain in Europe very long. Edith Steiner Kraus and Alice Herz Sommer presented several highly successful recitals in Czechoslovakia, but in the late 1940s they pursued their careers in the newly established state of Israel.

Prague native Alice Herz Sommer (born 1903) received her musical education at the German Academy of Music as well as with the Czech pianist and musicologist Václav Štěpán. Even before the war, she had appeared frequently as a recitalist and soloist with orchestras in Czechoslovakia, Germany, and Sweden. Her career, actually thriving during her stay in Terezín, went on after the war mainly in Czechoslovakia until 1949, when she emigrated to Israel with her young son, Raphael. Her husband died of typhus in Dachau shortly before the German surrender. For the next twenty years, Alice Herz Sommer gave countless recitals in her newly adopted homeland, where she joined the piano faculty at the Academy of Music in Jerusalem. Her son, Raphael, the "Sparrow" from *Brundibár*, established himself as a concert cellist and now resides in London. He has given several recitals there in collaboration with his mother.

The pianist Edith Steiner Kraus, born in Vienna in 1913 of Czech parentage, had a very similar fate. Her family moved back to Czechoslovakia, where the five-year-old Edith started her musical studies. As a child prodigy of eleven, she substituted for an absent guest artist as piano soloist with orchestra, having in her repertoire concertos by Mozart and Beethoven. Following her studies with Arthur Schnabel at the Berliner Hochschule für Musik, she came to Prague and launched a very successful career. In the summer of 1942, she and her husband, Karel Steiner, were deported to Terezín. She was the only one to survive the ordeal and returned to her activities as recitalist and soloist on the Prague radio. In 1949, she emigrated to Israel with her second husband, Arpad Bloedy, and became a teacher at the Academy of Music of the University of Tel-Aviv. Her teaching obligations did not stop her from extensive concertizing.

Active in Israel also was Tella Polák, who died there in 1971. The other surviving pianists pursued their interrupted work in the field of popular music. Kurt Maier moved to the United States, where he divided his activities between New York City and the so-called "Borscht circuit" in the Catskill Mountains. For some fifteen years he was featured as a piano entertainer at the Regency Hotel in New York, until his death on April 2, 1981, in North Yonkers, New York.

Martin Roman worked successfully in Las Vegas before settling down in the New York area, where he is in great demand as solo pianist and in a team with his wife Inge, soprano soloist and voice teacher. During his stay in America, Roman has made about a dozen LP records as arranger and pianist. Of special interest among them are the arrangements for the German version of the musical *Fiddler on the Roof*, in an apt translation by another former Terezín inmate, Henry Wegener; and the arrangements for the record featuring the tenor Fredy Haber, also a one-time unwilling Terezín resident.

The pianist Wolfgang Lederer allegedly found employment in Turkey, while the violinist Otto Sattler remained in Czechoslovakia playing in the Prague nightclubs. However, according to some sources, he too changed his domicile and in the early 1970s moved to West Germany.

Karel Berman was not the only successful singer of Terezín reputation. His friend Hanuš Thein (born in 1904) had a career of more than four decades on the stage of the National Theater in Prague. Simultaneously with his studies in law at the Charles University in Prague he attended the Prague Conservatory, where he took voice lessons with Egon Fuchs. In 1927 began his association with the National Theater, first as basso-buffo and, from 1932 onward, as a stage director also. Being silenced for a few years during the Nazi occupation, he returned to his work after the war and added extra duties to his schedule by teaching operatic acting at the Prague Conservatory in 1951. In 1964 he was named assistant director of the National Theater, a post which he held until his death in 1974.

The career of the tenor, David Grünfeld, actually started in Terezín. Born in Užhorod (Ruthenia) in 1915, in his youth he moved to Prague, where he pursued his musical studies until the outbreak of the hostilities. After the war, he utilized his extensive experience from Terezín in the United States, singing under the name of David Garen. He became a member of the National Broadcasting Company Opera, appeared as soloist with orchestras, such as the Boston and Pittsburgh Symphony, and made classical recordings. In 1961, he took up the position of a cantor at the Huntington (Long Island) Jewish Center, but he died there about two years later, in 1963.

A Viennese native, Anny Frey (born 1906), participated mainly in the Terezín cabarets. She had spent most of her life before the war in Czechoslovakia, and after her return there she was hired as a singer in the theater in Teplice, in Northern Bohemia.

The sojourn in Terezín influenced the lifestyle of Alexander Singer. Although originally from Rumania, he had lived before the war in Prague, working as a tailor. Thanks to his beautiful voice, he got a chance to participate in the Terezín operatic productions, and that, in turn, led him after the war to join the chorus of the Grand Opera in Prague. An appearance as a minor soloist with the Czech Philharmonic resulted in his engagement as a cantor in Johannesburg, South Africa.

From the younger generation, Greta Hoffmeister, one of the *Brundibár* stars, was only fifteen when she emerged from the concentration camp. She was united with her parents living in Israel. She received her education there and devoted her life to music, singing in the Academic Chorus in Jerusalem. One of her partners from *Brundibár*, Zdeněk Ornest, is an actor in a Prague theater.

Although not a musician, Vlasta Schönová should be mentioned because of her involvement in the musical production of *Fireflies*. For many years now, she has been well known through out Israel as an actress in the Haifa Theater under the name of Nava Shan.

Finally, one name must not be omitted, that of Zuzana Růžičková. In Terezín she was a young music enthusiast who never missed an opportunity to attend a concert or operatic performance. Born in Plzeň (Pilsen) in 1928, she started taking piano lessons there, but only after four years of incarceration in the concentration camps was she able to enter the Academy of Musical Arts in Prague. She graduated from the piano class, but her interest focused on the harpsichord to such an extent that today she is one of the most celebrated harpsichord virtuosos and recording artists in the world.

A number of other musicians, professionals, and amateurs lived to see the liberation. However, after the war they abandoned the musical field for various reasons. If the achievements of the aforementioned artists can be any criterion, then the annihilation of the others, multiplied by the number of all concentration camps, certainly caused an irreparable loss for all mankind, far beyond the wildest imagination.

NINETEEN

Evaluation of the Musical Activities in Terezín

Artistic and especially musical life in the Terezín concentration camp does not have any analogy in the history of the Third Reich. True, Terezín was not the only place where music was played and composed behind barbed wire. In the Warsaw ghetto, an entire symphony orchestra gave concerts under the baton of Szymon Pullmann.[56] The conductor and the majority of his musicians were killed in Treblinka. In the fall of 1942, the phenomenal young singer Marysia Ajzensztat[57] was murdered by the SS during the "liquidation campaign." This "Nightingale of the Ghetto" often sang as soloist with Pullmann's symphony orchestra and with a smaller ensemble, conducted by her father. Vocal music had been offered by several choral groups; among them was one of

---

[56]The same person is sometimes mentioned as Simon Pulver.
[57]Also spelled Maryasha Eisenstadt.

unusually high quality, the children's chorus, directed by Israel Fajwiszys.

In the Vilna ghetto, the Jewish Council organized a musical contest as late as 1943. An eleven-year-old boy, Alex Volkoviski, was awarded the second prize for his song *Stile, Stile,* written to the lyrics of S. Kacerginski. The song so impressed the composer Abraham Slep that he incorporated it into his own cantata, which he then performed in the ghetto. Many folksongs emerged from the ghettos and concentration camps. Not surprisingly, they used Yiddish texts, because that was the language spoken by the more than three million Jews living in occupied Poland and the Baltic States. The events of everyday life, the tragedy and despair as well as resistance and hope, were sung out in countless songs and ballads. Folk poets composed simple melodies or adapted new lyrics to well known popular tunes and folk songs.

Not even the most horrible concentration camps were left without music. The inmates of Buchenwald had the opportunity to hear a string quartet led by the famous French violinist Maurice Hewitt and another one in which Karel Fröhlich had for his partner his countryman, the violinist Jaroslav Pekelský. Chamber music resounded equally in Flossenbürg, where the Czech violinist Zdeněk Kolářský[58] performed Beethoven's sonatas with his compatriot Josef Kyselka at the piano. In the all-male camp Gleiwitz I., near Auschwitz, a small orchestra played semiclassical music. On one occasion they even went on a "concert tour" to the neighboring all-female camp, Gleiwitz II. As a welcome reward, they could spend a few precious moments in the company of equally lonely girls. And in Auschwitz the conditions were so morbid that a band had to play while the condemned prisoners were being led to their doom in the gas chambers. Then there was an orchestra consisting entirely of Jewish women and led by Alma Rosé, a niece of Gustav Mahler, which performed for the entertainment of Himmler, Dr. Mengele, and other SS officers.

The great accomplishment of the composers of serious music in Terezín had its equivalents in other concentration camps and

[58]Professor Kolářský was the violin teacher of the author at the Prague Conservatory of Music.

prisons, not necessarily Jewish. The great French composer Olivier Messiaen spent two years in a prison camp at Görlitz, Silesia. There he composed a *Quatuor pour la fin du temps* (Quartet for the end of time), for violin, clarinet, cello, and piano, and he himself played the piano part in the premiere, which took place in the camp on January 15, 1941.

The Czech composer Rudolf Karel was incarcerated for about two years in a Prague prison in the city district called Pankrác, and for one month at the Terezín Small Fortress, where he died of dysentery on March 6, 1945. At the time of his arrest, Karel was already sixty-one years old (born 1880 in Plzen) and suffering with heart trouble. This did not stop him from intensive creative work, first in the prison cell and then in a prison hospital. The guards and the prison physician smuggled to him pieces of neatly folded toilet paper, lined with music staff, on which he then wrote fragments of his new compositions. These were collected and secretly taken out of the premises for safekeeping. This way, without an overall view of the work, Karel composed a Nonet for flute, aboe, clarinet, bassoon, French horn, violin, viola, cello, and double bass, and in six months he wrote the whole opera, *Three Hairs of Old Wise Man*. Both compositions had to be edited, and the opera orchestrated, before their respective premieres in Prague after the war. Besides these major works, Karel wrote also several small pieces both in Pankrác and in Terezín.

In view of all these achievements, what makes the musical life in the Terezín ghetto so different and unique? The answer, in its great complexity, could be summarized in one simple word: everything.

The purpose and the history of the Terezín ghetto stamped its imprint on the life there, right from the beginning. The subsequent changeover to a model prison camp further influenced not only the life but the cultural activities as well. As has already been mentioned, Terezín was originally a gathering point for the Czech Jews before their final deportation to the extermination camps, and only later did it host a relatively small number of Jews from other European countries, mostly prominent people, who enjoyed somewhat privileged treatment. Most of these people belonged to the ranks of intelligentsia, and as such not only felt the urge to express

Cellist. Drawing by Otto Ungar.

Saxophonist. Drawing by Otto Ungar.

themselves intellectually, but also felt the need for spiritual food offered by their peers. In the field of music, these offerings were made in the form of musical presentations from the standard repertoire, supplemented by pieces of music written in the ghetto by the imprisoned composers.

Although the basic idea for the cultural activities in Terezín was to keep some semblance of normality, prevent stagnation, educate, and, yes, even entertain and let the inmates forget their grievous lot, the reasons of the individual artists for their involvement in their work were as varied as their personalities. Some did it for material advantages, others because they just could not comprehend that they were not living in normal circumstances. Some used the opportunity to satisfy their vanity, others had been driven by a sincere need for artistic manifestation. And yet they all had one thing in common: they hoped to return one day to their homes and resume their normal lives, as if awakening from a bad dream. The stay in Terezín and the subsequent camps had to be used therefore in such a way that the damage would be minimal and the advantage maximal.

Through the performance and creation of new works, the artists were maintaining their artistic standard and abilities on a professional level. This was further facilitated if the artist could obtain a position with the *Freizeitgestaltung,* and thus could avoid less desirable menial work and could devote all his energy to his chosen field. In this respect, the young people had the greatest opportunity, so much so that some of them really enjoyed their sojourn in Terezín. For the first time, they lived without parental supervision and guidance, for the first time they fell in love, for the first time they became involved in serious music-making, for the first time in their young lives they could be truly themselves. These exciting feelings could not be dampened by the unpleasantness and difficulties of the life in the ghetto.

It is practically impossible for an outsider to comprehend the complexities and significance of an imprisonment in a concentration camp. It is even more difficult to understand how such living conditions influence the sensitive soul of an artist. Instead of a weak attempt to evaluate the musical activities in Terezín, let us listen to the words of one of the most important performers there, the violinist Karel Fröhlich:

> For an artist, it was a tremendous opportunity to work during the war in his own field, with excellent colleagues, and actually, in a certain sense, in an ideal *milieu*. We did not have to do anything but play music. However, the philosophy of it was that we were not actually playing for the public, because the public always disappeared. In a sense, it was only an effort to get through this war, to survive, and then to continue under normal conditions. It was ideal in a way, but nevertheless the conditions were still abnormal, because you never knew if you would be sitting here tomorrow or if you would depart with one of those trains. So in one sense it was ideal, and in another sense it was abnormal. We all knew it, and we made the best of it. For example, when the soloist is concertizing, he always has problems—here in America, with renting of the hall, advertising, pianist; that all costs a lot of money. There we could play a recital twenty or thirty times to perfection. We did not have to pay for it, and we lived in relative security. However, in the end we were deported to Auschwitz.
>
> So, very often I realized that before the war we had Bronislaw Hubermann visiting Prague. He came there every year, and every year he had the same audiences, audiences which came to the "Lucerna" hall to hear him. We had a different audience for every performance. A transport of a thousand people arrived, and a thousand of people departed. And we looked at it always and said: "This is Terezín, this is a concentration camp, and even if we have the opportunity here to play and practice now, to play in public—"in public" was rather relative—it is nevertheless very abnormal, and it is not a complete reality. It is an abnormal state." . . . I played there for dead audiences. . . . For the survivors it had some sense. . . .
>
> Now I will tell you something subjectively. I practiced in Terezín more than in civilian life. I woke up often at three o'clock in the morning, at four I started practicing in some office the entire violin repertoire: concertos by Brahms, Tchaikovsky, Sibelius, Mendelssohn, Bruch, Wieniawski, Paganini. And I said to myself in October 1944 that now, when the war was at its end—because we knew already that the Americans were in France and in the Netherlands—I was

altogether prepared for a solo career. And at that moment I was deported to Auschwitz, and I had a lot of time, for a change, when I did not practice. But it was good in a sense. I was prepared, and when I returned from Buchenwald to Prague several months later, I had an audition there for the position of concertmaster in an opera house, and I got the appointment. So, I did not forget everything completely. For me personally, subjectively, being there (in Terezín) and being able to practice there had the advantage that immediately after the war I could start as concertmaster in the opera. However, that was also not completely normal. It was very abnormal."[59]

Compared to the practical statement of Karel Fröhlich, Viktor Ullmann had a more sophisticated view of his stay in Terezín and its effects on his own artistic growth:

> ... Thus, Goethe's maxim: "Live within the moment, live in eternity" has always revealed to me the enigmatic meaning of Art. ... Theresienstadt was and is for me the school of Form. Earlier, when one did not feel the impact and burden of material life, because they were erased by comfort, this magic accomplishment of civilization, it was easy to create beautiful forms. Here, where even in daily life one must overcome matter by the power of the form, where anything connected with the Muses is in utter contrast to the surroundings, here is the true school for masters, if one, following Schiller, perceives the secret of every work of art in the endeavor to annihilate matter by the means of form, which, presumably, is the overall mission of man, not only of the esthetical man, but of the ethical man as well. I have written in Theresienstadt a fair amount of new music, mainly to meet the needs and wishes of conductors, stage directors, pianists, and singers, and thereby the Recreation Administration (*Freizeitgestaltung*) of the ghetto. To compile a list would seem as superfluous as to point out that piano playing was impossible in Theresienstadt as long as there were no instruments. Likewise uninteresting for the future generations should be the painful scarcity of manuscript paper.

[59]Transcribed from a taped interview with the author on December 2, 1973, in New York.

However, it must be emphasized that Theresienstadt has served to *enhance,* not to impede, my musical activities, that by no means did we sit weeping on the banks of the waters of Babylon, and that our endeavor with respect to Arts was commensurate with our will to live. And I am convinced that all those who, in life and in art, were fighting to force from upon resisting matter, will agree with me."[60]

Eloquent, momentous words! However, can they match the words of Greta Hofmeister, the "Aninka" from the Terezín productions of *Brundibár,* when she exclaimed exuberantly:
"Music! Music *was* life!"

---

[60]Statement of Viktor Ullmann, as quoted in Dr. H. G. Adler's book *Theresienstadt 1941–1945,* in the translation of Max Bloch; used with the permission of both gentlemen.

Relaxation in the sick bay. Drawing by Malva Schalek.

Concert hall in Magdeburg Barracks. Drawing by Bedřich Fritta.

Epilogue

The rock of Vyšehrad (High Castle), towering on the right bank over the Vltava river (Moldau) in Prague, has a special place in the heart of every Czech. From here the first Czech rulers reigned over their tribe; from here, in the midst of her vision, Duchess Libuše, according to a legend, voiced the famous prophecy: "My Czech nation will never perish, the terrors of hell it will successfully withstand." From here she founded the proud capital of the country. The remaining witnesses of the old glory are today a few ruins of the ancient castle and the almost thousand-year-old rotund chapel of St. Martin.

It was not an accident that this location had been selected as a burial site for the most beloved and most respected sons and daughters of the Czech nation. Poets, writers, politicians, and scientists lie here in one accord with artists and musicians. Smetana's grave is here, and so is Dvořák's. The greatest honor was granted to the selected few who were laid to rest in the prominently located mausoleum "Slavín." An inspiring message engraved on its top greets the visitors of the cemetery: "Although They died, They are still speaking."

In vain would one search for the names of Krása, Haas, Klein, or Ledeč in Vysehrad. Their ashes and those of their colleagues from Terezín are scattered around Auschwitz and Kauffering or were carried away on the waves of Ohře and Labe perhaps all the way to the Atlantic. However, they are speaking to us. They are pointing out to us with accusing fingers the terrible consequences of moral decay. They are speaking to us about human dignity and the sacredness of life even in the midst of unimaginable misery; they are

199

speaking about the courage of the unbending, unyielding human spirit. And above all through the tones of the Terezín composers, spurted out of their sorrow and anguish, they speak to us about the eternal hope for a better tomorrow.

Are we listening?

Existing Compositions
Written in Terezín

Berman, Karel: *Poupata*—Four Songs for Bass & Piano (Czech)
Terezín—Suite for Piano
Three Songs for High Voice & Piano (Czech)

Domažlický, František: *May Song* for Men's Chorus (Czech)
Song Without Words for String Quartet

Grünfeld-Z. Schul: *Uv'tzeil K'nofecho* for String Quartet

Haas, Pavel: *Al S'fod* for Men's Chorus
Study for String Orchestra
Four Songs to the Text of Chinese Poetry for Bass
& Piano (Czech)

Klein, Gideon: *Trio* for Violin, Viola & Cello
Fantasia and Fugue for String Quartet
Sonata for Piano
Madrigal (text by F. Villon) for 2 Sopranos, Alto,
Tenor & Bass (Czech)
Madrigal (text by F. Hölderlin) for 2 Sopranos,
Alto, Tenor & Bass (Czech)
Old Folk Poetry for Men's Chorus (Czech)

arranged: *Wiegenlied* for Soprano & Piano (Hebrew)
Bachuri Leantisa for Women's Chorus (Hebrew)

Kohn, Viktor: *Praeludium* for String Quartet

Krása, Hans: *Brundibár*—Children's Opera, full score and vocal
score (Czech, English)
Passacaglia and Fugue for Violin, Viola & Cello

201

	Dance for Violin, Viola & Cello
	Theme with Variations for String Quartet
	Three Songs for Baritone, Clarinet, Viola & Cello (Czech)
Ledeč, Egon:	*Gavotte* for String Quartet
Schul, Zikmund:	*Schicksal*—Song for Alto, Flute, Viola & Cello (German)
	Two Chassidic Dances for Viola & Cello
	Duo for Violin & Viola
	Finale from *Cantana Judaica* for Men's Chorus & Tenor Solo (Hebrew)
Taube, Carlo:	*Ein Jüdisches Kind* for Soprano & Piano (German)
Ullmann, Viktor:	*Third String Quartet*
	Sonata No. 5 for Piano
	Sonata No. 6 for Piano
	Sonata No. 7 for Piano
	Der Kaiser von Atlantis—Opera, full score and vocal score (German, English)
	Three Songs for Baritone and Piano
	Herbst for Voice, Violin, Viola & Cello (German)
	Der Mensch und sein Tag for Voice & Piano (German)
	Two Chinese Songs for Voice & Piano (German)
	Hölderlin Lieder for Voice & Piano (German)
	Brezulinka—Three Songs for Voice & Piano (Yiddish)
	Wendla im Garten for Voice & Piano (German)
	Abendphantasie for Voice & Piano (German)
	Immer in Mitten for Mezzo-soprano & Piano (German)
	Chansons des Enfants Française for Voice & Piano (French)
	Three Songs for Children's Chorus (Hebrew)
	Three Songs for Women's Chorus (Yiddish)
	Two Songs for Women's Chorus (Hebrew)
	Three Songs for Men's Chorus (Yiddish)
	Two Songs for Mixed Chorus (Hebrew)
Weber, Ilse:	*Seven Songs* for Alto & Piano (German, Czech)

Copies of these compositions, with the exception of the full score of Ullmann's *Der Kaiser von Atlantis,* are in the possession of Joža Karas.

Biographical Sketches

Ančerl, Karel, conductor, born April 11, 1908, in Tučapy (Southern Bohemia). He graduated from the Prague Conservatory in conducting and composition. He became conductor at the Liberated Theater and at the Czechoslovak Radio in Prague. After his imprisonment he returned to the Radio Orchestra in Prague, then became conductor of the Grand Opera of May 5th, and finally, in 1950, the music director of the Czech Philharmonic. From 1969 until his death on July 3, 1973, he conducted the Toronto Symphony. As a guest conductor, he appeared with major orchestras around the world and, also, made a large number of recordings from the Czech as well as world repertoire.

Arányi, Juliette, pianist, born December 19, 1912, in Brezno (Slovakia), died in Auschwitz in 1944. She studied piano in Bratislava and Vienna and started concertizing as a child prodigy at the age of six. Viktor Ullmann dedicated his Piano Concerto, Op. 25 to her.

Berman, Karel, basso, born April 14, 1919, in Jindřichův Hradec (Bohemia). He graduated from the Prague Conservatory after his release from concentration camps, majoring in voice and stage directing. He worked in both capacities in opera houses in Opava and Plzeň (Pilsen), and since 1953, he has been a member of the National Theater in Prague. He is very active in the field of recording and television, including an appearance on CBS-TV in 1971, and sang on operatic and concert stages throughout Europe and in Japan.

Brock, Robert, conductor, born May 27, 1905, in Rakovník (Bohemia). After studies at the Prague Conservatory, he was engaged in Switzerland, Germany, Russia, and Prague. In 1945 he became conductor in Brno, then at the Grand Opera of May 5th in Prague and, finally, at the National Theater. He was professor of conducting at the Academy of Musical Arts in Prague from 1948 until his retirement in 1974. He died in Prague on December 2, 1979.

Deutsch, Peter, composer and conductor, born September 18, 1901, in Berlin. He wrote music for German films until 1929, when he moved to Denmark. There he composed music for many Danish films, theater and radio, as well as several solo and orchestral works, sometimes under the pseudonym, Pete Alman. After his return from Terezín, he resumed his activities in Copenhagen as composer and conductor of student orchestras. He died there on May 13, 1965.

Freudenfeld, Rudolf, educator, born September 23, 1921, in Prague. In Terezín, he conducted all fifty-five performances of Krása's children opera, *Brundibár*. After the war, he returned to his original field and became a principal of a secondary school in Prague. He changed his name to Franěk.

Fröhlich, Karel, violinist, born November 20, 1917, in Olomouc (Moravia). While a student at the Prague Conservatory and the Master School, he concertized in Czechoslovakia. Immediately after the liberation, he became concertmaster at the Grand Opera of May 5th in Prague, and in that capacity he left for Paris to pursue his studies at he "L'École Normale." He made extensive tours of France and Belgium, and in 1948 he came to the United States, where he continued concertizing with his wife, Françoise Dupuy-Fröhlich.

Grünfeld, David, tenor, born in Užhorod (Ruthenia) in 1915. Before the war he studied singing in Prague. In 1946 he emigrated to the United States, where he sang under the name David Garen as a soloist with various orchestras, member of the NBC Opera, and finally, as a cantor in Huntington (L.I.). He died there on June 6, 1963.

Haas, Pavel, composer, born June 21, 1899, in Brno. He graduated from the Conservatory and Master School in Brno, where he was one of the best students of Leoš Janáček. A very versatile composer, he wrote music for films and stage plays as well as orchestral, choral, solo, and chamber works. He died in Auschwitz on October 17, 1944.

Herz-Sommer, Alice, pianist, born November 26, 1903 in Prague. She studied at the German Music Academy in Prague. She performed in numerous recitals and as soloist in Czechoslovakia, Germany and Sweden. After the liberation, she resumed her concertizing in several European countries and in Israel, where she took up residence in 1949. She became also teacher at the Music Academy in Jerusalem.

Kaff, Bernard, pianist, born May 14, 1905, in Brno. He studied in Brno, Vienna and Berlin and concertized in a number of Europan countries, often featuring contemporary music. For more than a decade he commuted between Vienna and Brno, teaching piano. He died in Auschwitz on October 17, 1944.

Klein, Gideon, pianist and composer, born December 6, 1919, in Přerov (Moravia). After his graduation from the Master School in Prague, in 1939, as a pianist, he studied composition with Alois Hába. His great talent was, however, surpressed by the ban on performances by Jewish artists, and his subsequent internment in several concentration camps. He died about January 27, 1945, in Fürstengrube.

Kling, Pavel (Paul), violinist, born in Opava in 1928. He started his solo career as a child prodigy, while pursuing his studies in Brno, Vienna, and finally, in Prague, where he graduated from the Academy of Musical Arts. He spent several years in Japan as a concertmaster and string quartet player. Subsequently, he became concertmaster of the Louisville Symphony and violin teacher at the University of Louisville, Kentucky. At the present time, he teaches at the University of Victoria, British Columbia.

Krása, Hans, composer, born November 30, 1899 in Prague. Before his graduation from the German Music Academy in Prague, in 1921, he was engaged as vocal coach at the German Theater in Prague. He started writing music before he reached his tenth birthday. He was not very prolific, but most of his compositions have been published in Paris and Vienna and performed in various European cities. He died in Auschwitz on October 17, 1944.

Ledeč, Egon, violinist, born March 16, 1889, in Kostelec nad Orlicí (Eastern Bohemia). He graduated from the Prague Conservatory in 1906, and two years later he joined the Czech Philharmonic. After a stint in the Army and several engagements in Slovakia, he rejoined the Czech Philharmonic in 1926, and the following year he was promoted to the post of associate concertmaster, which he held until 1939. He was active as soloist and chamber music player as well as composer of a number of salon pieces. He perished in Auschwitz on October 17, 1944.

Pappenheim, Leo, conductor, born August 13, 1896 in Amsterdam. He studied at the Conservatory of Cologne under Hermann Abendroth. He made his conducting debut in 1916 and two years later was appointed to the Municipal Theater in Wupperthal. Consequently, he became associated with a number of German opera companies and orchestras. Because of the Nazi regime, he returned to Holland as conductor of the Dutch Operaensemble in Rotterdam and in 1939 he took over the leadership of the Arnhem Orchestral Society (after the war named the Gelders Orchestra). He resumed this post after the incarceration in Terezín and remained there until 1961. He continued conducting various orchestras in Holland and in Germany until 1975. He died in Arnhem on August 30, 1982.

Reiner, Karel, composer, and pianist, born June 27, 1910 in Žatec (Western Bohemia). He studied law and musicology at the Prague University and graduated from the Master School in composition. As a pianist, he propagated contemporary music throughout Europe and was very active in various musical organizations. Many of his compositions reveal his strong political (Communist) affiliation. He died in Prague on October 17, 1979.

Růžičková, Zuzana, harpsichordist, born January 14, 1928 in Pizeň. She studied at the Academy of Musical Arts in Prague from 1947 until 1951. The same year, she started teaching there together with embarking on a concert and recording career which led her to the ranks of the foremost virtuosi of her instrument.

Schächter, Rafael, conductor and pianist, born May 27, 1905, in Braila (Rumania). After WW I, he came to Brno, where he started his musical studies and later continued at the Prague Conservatory, where he graduated in composition and conducting, and at the Master School in piano. He formed a very successful Chamber Music Opera and was a sought after vocal coach. He died in Auschwitz on October 17, 1944.

Schul, Zikmund (Siegmund), composer, born January 11, 1916, in Kassell (Germany). He sought refuge in Prague, where he studied with Alois Hába. He was very interested and influenced by the Hebraic chant, as witnessed by all his works written in Terezín. He died there on June 20, 1944.

Simon, James, musicologist and composer, born September 29, 1880, in Berlin. He was a student of Conrad Ansorge (piano) and Max Bruch (composition). From 1907 until 1919, he taught at the Klindworth-Scharwenka Conservatory in Berlin. In 1934 he moved to Zurich and later to Amsterdam, where he was arrested in 1941. He died in Auschwitz in 1944.

Steiner Kraus, Edith, pianist, born in Vienna in 1913. She lived in Bohemia, where she began performing at the age of eleven. Following her studies with Schnabel in Berlin, she moved to Prague and played frequently on the Czechoslovak Radio. After the war, she emigrated to Israel and there she resumed her career as performer and teacher at the Rubin Academy in Tel-Aviv.

Taube, Carlo S., pianist and composer, born July 4, 1897, in Galicia. He studied piano with Busoni in Vienna, but for economic reasons he played in night clubs in Brno and Prague. He died in Auschwitz in October, 1944.

Thein, Hanuš, basso and stage director, born January 17, 1904, in Pardubice (Bohemia). Before completing his studies at the Prague Conservatory, he was engaged by the National Theater in Prague, in 1927, mainly as basso-buffo, and he started directing in 1932. After a short imprisonment in Terezín, he returned to the theater and also began to teach operatic acting at the Prague Conservatory. He died in Prague on December 30, 1974.

Ullmann, Viktor, composer, born January 1, 1898 in Těšín (Silesia). He studied with Arnold Schoenberg in Vienna and quarter-tone composition with Alois Hába at the Prague Conservatory. He became conductor at the New German Theater in Prague and, in 1927, director of the opera house in Ústí (Aussig). After several short stays in Zurich, Vienna, Stuttgart, etc., he returned to Prague. He privately published many of his prewar compositions. He died in Auschwitz on October 17, 1944.

Bibliography

Books and Articles

Adler, H.G. *Theresienstadt 1941–1945*. 2nd Ed. Tübingen: J. C. B. Mohr (Paul Siebeck), 1960

——.*Die Verheimlichte Wahrheit* (The Concealed Truth). Tübingen; J. C. B. Mohr (Paul Siebeck), 1958

Apel, Willi. *Harvard Dictionary of Music*. Cambridge, Mass.: Harvard University Press, 1969

Baker's Biographical Dictionary of Musicians. 5th Ed. revised by Nicolas Slonimsky. New York: G. Schirmer, 1971

Beckson, Karl and Ganz, Arthur. *A Reader's Guide to Literary Terms*. New York: The Noonday Press, 1960

Bloch, Max. "Viktor Ullmann—A Brief Biography and Appreciation," in *Journal of the Arnold Schoenberg Institute*, III/2, Los Angeles, October 1979

Bor, Josef. *The Terezín Requiem*. New York: Alfred A. Knopf, 1963

Caro, Klara. *Experiences in Theresienstadt* (Testimony). Yad Vashem Archives, Jerusalem

——.*Paul Eppstein in Theresienstadt* (Testimony). Yad Vashem Archives, Jerusalem

Černušák, Gracián, Štědroň, Bohumír, Nováček, Zdenko. *Česko-slovenský Hudební Slovník Osob a Institucí* (Czechoslovak Musical Dictionary of Persons and Institutions), 2 Vols. Prague: Státní Hudební Vydavatelství, 1963

Červinková, Blanka. *Johann Krása, život a dílo* (Johann Krása, his life and work). Ms. written for Joža Karas. Prague, 1972

... *I Never Saw Another Butterfly* ... (edited by Hana Volavková), New York: McGraw-Hill, 1962

Collective of Authors: *Dějiny Československa v datech* (The History of Czechoslovakia in dates). Prague: Svoboda, 1968

"David Garen." (Obituary). in *The New York Times,* June 8, 1963

Ems, Hedwig. *Theresienstadt 1939–1945* (Testimony). Yad Vashem Archives, Jerusalem

Feder, Richard. *Židovská Tragedie* (The Jewish Tragedy). Kolín: Lusk, 1949

Felix, Václav: "Composer Karel Reiner Died," in *Music News from Prague,* No. 9–10,1979, Prague, December, 1979

Fénelon, Fania. *Playing for Time.* New York: Atheneum, 1977

Fischel, Hanka Hoffmann. *Das kulturelle Leben und die erzieherische Tätigkeit in Ghetto Theresienstadt 1941–1945 und im Familienlager der Juden aus Theresienstadt in Auschwitz 1943–1944* (The cultural life and the educational activities in the Terezín Ghetto 1941–1945 and in the family camp of the Jews from Terezín in Auschwitz 1943–1944). Transcript of a taped interview in Mordechaj, 1965. Archives of the Hebrew University, Jerusalem

Green, Gerald. *The Artists of Terezín.* New York: Hawthorne Books, 1969

Helfert, Vladimír and Steinhard, Erich. *Die Musik in der Tschechoslowakischen Republik* (Music in the Czechoslovak Republic). Prague: Orbis, 1938

Herrmann(ová)-Lewis, Helena. *Testimony.* Ms. Belfast, August 1977

Hilberg, Raul. *Destruction of the European Jews.* Chicago: Quadrangle Books, 1961

Hoffmeister, Adolf. *Hry a protihry* (Plays and counter-plays). Prague: Orbis, 1963

―――. *Hry z avantgardy* (Plays from the avant-garde). Prague: Orbis, 1963

Holde, Artur. *Jews in Music—From the Age of Enlightenment to the Present,* New edition prepared by Irene Heskes. New York: Bloch Publishing Company, 1974

Hostomská, Anna. *Opera.* Prague: Státní nakladatelství krásné literatury, hudby a umění, 1956

Iltis, Rudolf. "Dne 20. ledna 1962 bude tomu 20 let" (On January 20, 1962 it will be twenty years), in *Židovská ročenka 5722 (1961–62)*

(Jewish Yearbook 5722). Prague: Rada židovských náboženských obcí, 1962

Jacobsohn, Jakob. *From Berlin to Theresienstadt 1943–1945* (Testimony). Yad Vashem Archives, Jerusalem

Karas, Joža. *Jewish Music during the Nazi Occupation*. Ms. Bloomfield, Conn., 1974

————."Music in Terezín," in *Journal of Synagogue Music*, Vol 5, No. 1. New York: Cantors Assembly, October 1973

————."The Holocaust in Music," in *Proceedings—Third Philadelphia Conference*, Philadelphia Conference on Teaching the Holocaust, Philadelphia, 1977

"Karel Ančerl" (obituary), in *International Musician*, October 1973

Kulišová, Táňa; Lagus, Karel; Polák, Josef. *Terezín*. Prague: Nase Vojsko, 1967

Kulka, Otto Dov. *Bericht über das "Theresienstadter Familienlager" in Auschwitz-Birkenau* (Account of the "Terezín family camp" in Auschwitz-Birkenau), 1964; Archives of the Hebrew University, Jerusalem

Kuna, Milan. "Music—Its Ethical Power," in *Arts in Terezín 1941– 1945*, Memorial Terezín—The Small Fort, 1973

Lagus, Karel and Polák, Josef. *Město za mřížemi* (Town behind bars). Prague: Naše Vojsko, 1964

Ledeč, Egon. *Letters from Terezín*. Photocopies of originals from the collection of Dr. Jan Ledeč in Prague

Liebmann, Herbert. "In den KZ Entstandende Kompositionen— Uraufführung in München" (Compositions originated in concentration camps—premiere in Munich), in *Düsseldorfer Allgemeine Zeitung*, spring 1973 (exact date not available)

Ludvová, Jitka. "Viktor Ullmann 1898–1944," in *Hudební Věda* (Musicology), XVI/2, Prague, 1979

Lustig, Arnošt. *Night and Hope*. Iowa City: The University of Iowa, 1972

Mandl, Thomas (Tomáš). *Das kulturelle Leben und die erzieherische Tätigkeit im Ghetto Theresienstadt 1941–1945 und im Familienlager der Juden aus Theresienstadt in Auschwitz 1943–1944* (The cultural life and the educational activities in the Terezín ghetto 1941– 1945 and in the family camp of the Jews from Terezín in Auschwitz 1943–1944). Transcript of a taped interview in Köln,

West Germany, March 7, 1966. Archives of the Hebrew University, Jerusalem

Müllerová, Blanka. *Hans Krása*. Doctoral dissertation, Prague, 1966

_____*Hans Krása—Kapitoly ze života a díla skadatele* (Hans Krása—Chapters from the life and work of the composer). Original version of the doctoral dissertation, Prague, 1966

N. "Úděl Židů v době Protektorátu Čechy a Morava" (The lot of the Jews during the Protectorate Bohemia and Moravia), in *Katolík*, Chicago, March 5, 1974

Očadlík, Mirko. *Svět Orchestru—České orchestrální skladby* (The World of the Orchestra—Czech orchestral compositions). Prague: Orbis, 1944

Oppenhejm, Ralph. *An der Grenze des Lebens—Theresienstädter Tagebuch* (On the border of life—Terezín diary). Hamburg: Rütten & Loening Verlag, 1961

Pawetczyńska, Anna. *Wartości a Przemoc* (Values and violence). Warsaw: Państwowe Wydawnictwo Naukowe, 1973

Peduzzi, Lubomír. "Haasovské výroční rozjímání" (Haas' anniversary meditation), in *Hudební Rozhledy*, Vol. 19, Prague, 1969

_____*Pavel Haas a jeho tvorba za okupace* (Pavel Haas and his creative activity during the occupation). Doctoral dissertation, Brno, 1963

_____"Složeno v Terezín" (Composed in Terrezín), in *Hudební Rozhledy*, Vol. 6, Prague, 1968

_____"Vlastenecká symbolika posledních děl Pavla Haase" (The patriotic symbolism of the last works of Pavel Haas), *Sborník JAMU III.* (Yearbook JAMU III.) Brno, 1961

"Protifašistický večer" (Anti-fascist evening), in *Věstník Židovské Náboženské Obce*, XX/3, Prague, 1958

Rabinowitch, Israel. *Of Jewish Music Ancient and Modern*. Montreal: The Book Center, 1952

Ringelblum, Emanuel. "Cultural Activities in the Ghetto," in *The Warsaw Ghetto Uprising*, Congress for Jewish Culture, New York, 1975

Rubin, Ruth. *Voices of a People*. New York: McGraw-Hill, 1973

Saleski, Gdal. *Famous Musicians of Jewish Origin*. New York: Bloch Publishing Co., 1949

Schmiedt, Schlomo. "Hehalutz in Theresienstadt—Its Influence and Educational Activities," in *Yad Vashem Studies on the European Jewish Catastrophe and Resistance*, Vol. VII, Yad Vashem, Jerusalem, 1968

Shan, Nava. *Die erzieherische Tätigkeit im Ghetto Theresienstadt 1941– 1945 und im Familienlager der Theresienstadter Juden in Auschwitz 1943–1944* (Educational activities in the Terezín Ghetto 1941– 1945 and in the family camp of the Terezín Jews in Auschwitz 1943–1944). Transcript of a taped interview, 1965; Archives of the Hebrew University, Jerusalem

Shek, Zeev. *The Story of Theresienstadt* (short article), Theresienstadt Martyrs Remembrance Fund, Givat-Chaim Ichud, (signed by the author on January 4, 1977)

Slavický, Milan. *Gideon Klein*. Ms. written for Joža Karas, Prague, 1971.

_____."Gideon Klein-torso života a díla" (Gideon Klein—Torso of Life and Work), in *mudebni Věda* (Musicology) XIV/4, Prague, 1977

Sormorá, Eva. *Divadlo v Terezíně 1941-1945* (Theater in Terezín 1941- 1945), Ustí nad Labem, Severočeské Nakladatelství for Památník Terezín, 1973.

Terezín (memorial volume), edited by Fratišek Ehrmann, Otta Heitlinger, and Rudolf Iltis. Prague: Council of Jewish Religious Communities, Prague, 1965

Terezín Ghetto 1945, compiled by the Ministry of Social Welfare, Prague, 1945

The Jews in Czechoslovakia (Collection of essays by various authors). The Jewish Publication Society of America, Philadelphia, and Society for the History of Czechoslovak Jews, New York; Vol. 1, 1968; Vol. 2, 1971

Tihlaříková, Jaromíra. "Skladatelé v Terezíně" (Composers in Terezín), in *Hudební Rozhledy*, Vol. 23, Prague, 1968

Totenbuch Theresienstadt, Deportierte aus Österreich (Book of names of the dead from Terezín, Deported from Austria), compiled by Jüdisches Komitee für Theresienstadt, Vienna, 1971

Tuma, Mirko. "Memories of Theresienstadt," in *Performing Arts Journal*, Vol. 1., No. 2, New York, 1976

Ullmann, Viktor. *Reviews of Musical Performances in Terezín*, copies of originals from the collection of Dr. H. G. Adler, London

"Úmrtí" (Obituaries), in *Hudební Rozhledy*, vol. 2, Prague, 1980

Utitz, Emil. *Psychologie života v terezínském koncentračním táboře* (The Psychology of the life in the Terezín concentration camp). Prague: Dělnické Nakladatelství, 1947

Volavková, Hana. *Příběh židovského muzea v Praze* (The story of the Jewish museum in Prague), Prague: Odeon, 1966

Vrkočová, Ludmila. *Hudební místopis Čech* (The musical topography of Bohemia). Doctoral dissertation, Prague, 1970

Correspondence

Adler, H. G., London, May 17, 1973; June 16, 1973; December 20, 1976

Benda, Vilém, State Jewish Museum in Prague, March 23, 1971

Brock, Robert, Prague, January 26, 1972

de Jong, L., Netherlands State Institute for War Documentation, Amsterdam, January 20, 1978

Domažlický, František, Prague, June 24, 1973

Drori, Hana, Hachotrim, Israel, April 2, 1972

Glaser(ová) Eva, Caracas, Venezuela, March 10, 1973

Herz Sommer, Alice, Jerusalem, November 29, 1971

Herrmann(ová)-Lewis, Helen, Belfast, Northern Ireland, August 30, 1977; September 23, 1977

Hierck, H., Gelders Orchestra in Arnhem, Netherlands, March 25, 1983

Kirk, Käthie, Danish Composers' Society in Copenhagen, May 17, 1982

Klinke, Sephi, Nuremberg, December 16, 1973

Lagus, Karel, Prague, January 17, 1973

Leydensdorff, Hessel Hermann, Naarden, Netherlands, March 7, 1978

Mandl, Tomáš, Meerbusch, West Germany, June 23, 1977; February 2, 1979

May, Marianne, Pine Bush, New York, November 15, 1971; December 3, 1971; February 13, 1973

Peduzzi, Lubomír, Brno, Czechoslovakia, July 14, 1972

Pelleg, Inge, Haifa, June 18, 1972

Roman, Martin, Emerson, New Jersey, August 12, 1978

Shek, Alice, Jerusalem, May 30, 1979

Silberfeld, Margit, Jerusalem, October 25, 1977; May 25, 1977 (letter to Dr. Gretl Fischer)

Steiner Kraus, Edith (Mrs. Arpad Bloedy), Givataim, Israel, August 1, 1973

Vrba, Karel, Freiburg, West Germany, March 1977 (no date on the letter); February 25, 1977 (should read May)

Weber, Vilém, Prague, December 27, 1971

Wehle, Kurt, Floral Park, New York, April 1, 1973; April 22, 1973

Weiss, Arnošt, Prague, October 30, 1970

Taped Interviews

Adler, H. G., London, September 25–October 3, 1973 (2 tapes)

Ančerl, Karel, New York, January 10, 1972

Bacon, Yehuda, Jerusalem, January 4, 1977

Bloch, Schmuel (Jiří), Zikhron Ya'aqov, Israel, December 30, 1976

Dvořák, Doris, Boston, May 9, 1976

Fröhlich, Karel, New York, December 2, 1973 (2 tapes)

Hofmeister Herz, Greta, Jerusalem, January 7, 1977

Kantor, Alfred, Irvington-on-Hudson, New York, March 19, 1973

Kling, Pavel, Louisville, Kentucky, September 20, 1972 (taped letter)

Maier, Kurt, North Yonkers, New York, June 25, 1978 (2 tapes)

Mayer-Resheff, Eva, Jerusalem, January 5, 1977

Reiner, Karel, Prague, September 17, 1973

Roman, Martin, Emerson, New Jersey, September 8, 1978

Růžičková, Zuzana, Prague, January 11, 1977

Shan, Nava, Israel, December 29, 1976
Shek, Zeev, Jerusalem, January 5, 1977
Steiner-Kraus, Edith (Mrs. Arpad Bloedy), Tel-Aviv, December 29, 1976
Thein, Hanuš, Prague, September 22, 1973
Vidar, Max, Jerusalem, January 2, 1977

Index of Names

INDEX OF NAMES